SUCCESSFUL STAFF DEVELOPMENT

A How-To-Do-It Manual

Marcia Trotta

HOW-TO-DO-IT MANUALS FOR LIBRARIANS

NUMBER 55

NEAL-SCHUMAN PUBLISHERS, INC.
New York, London

Published by Neal-Schuman Publishers, Inc.
100 Varick Street
New York, NY 10013

Printed and bound in the United States of America.

Library of Congress Cataloging-in-Publication Data

Trotta, Marcia.
    Successful staff development : a how-to-do-it manual / Marcia
Trotta.
      p.   cm. -- (How-to-do-it manuals for librarians ; no. 55)
    Includes bibliographical references and index.
    ISBN 1-55570-180-9 (alk. paper)
    1. Library employees--In-service training--United States.
2. Librarians--In-service training--United States. 3. Public
libraries--United States--Personnel management. 4. Career
development--United States. I. Title. II. Series: How-do-do-it
manuals for libraries ; no. 55.
Z668.5.T76   1995
023'.8--dc20   95-32012

To the Staff of the

Meriden Public Library

It is an honor to work with you all.
I am proud to call you my colleagues,
but even prouder to call you my friends.

CONTENTS

Figures   **vii**

Preface   **ix**

1. What They Didn't Teach You in Library School   **1**

2. Beginning a Staff Development Program in Your Library   **9**

3. Developing Individual Potential in Your Library   **19**

4. Educating One Another   **31**

5. Mentoring as a Means of Staff Development   **39**

6. Day-to-Day Basics for Managers   **47**

7. Model Staff Development Programs   **57**

8. Evaluating Staff Performance   **89**

9. Beyond Salaries: Rewarding Effective Performance   **99**

10. Resources   **105**

Index   **111**

FIGURES

2.1   Program Plan: Staff Development/The Process   **15**

2.2   Needs Assessment: Leader Audit for Management   **16**

2.3   Needs Assessment: Training Needs Identification   **16**

2.4   Needs Assessment: Training Needs Survey   **17**

2.5   Seminar Purposes   **17**

3.1   Trainer Checklist   **29**

3.2   Sample Training Outline   **30**

4.1   Model Program   **36**

4.2   Sample Handout for Model Program   **37**

4.3   Sample Handout: Developing an Achievement Mentality   **37**

5.1   Mentor Survey   **43**

5.2   Hints for Being a Good Mentor   **44**

5.3   Characteristics of Good Mentors   **45**

7.1   Sample Training Outline   **59**

7.2   Communicating Effectively   **62**

7.3   Handout for Communication Training   **63**

7.4   Communication Handout   **64**

7.5   Organizational Communication Network   **65**

7.6   Training Curriculum   **67**

7.7   Handout: Getting the Most Out of Training   **70**

7.8   Handout: Welcome!   **71**

7.9   Teamwork   **71**

7.10 Teamwork Planning Wheel   **72**

7.11 Teamwork Handout: Thinking About Teamwork   **73**

7.12 Organizing Your Time   **75**

7.13 Time Management Handout   **76**

7.14 Time Management Handout: Setting Priorities   **76**

7.15 Work Schedule   **77**

7.16 Customer Service Handout   **80**

7.17 Customer Service Assessment   **81**

7.18 Sample Customer Services Policy   **82**

7.19 How to Apply Customer Service Techniques to
Service Goals   **85**

7.20 Sample Cases for Practicing Customer Service Skills   **86**

7.21 Things to Remember About Customer Service   **87**

8.1 Supervisor's Self-Evaluation Checklist   **94**

8.2 Checklist for Rating Employees   **95**

8.3 Employee Evaluation   **96**

8.4 Overcoming Employee Resistance to Change   **97**

8.5 Evaluation for Training Program   **97**

9.1 Ways to Give Recognition   **102**

9.2 Sample Opportunities to Provide Recognition   **103**

PREFACE

Successful Staff Development is about more than training our staffs. It is about the necessity of evaluating the public library services we are providing, and keeping them changing and growing to meet our community's needs. We must keep our staffs current on the best methods of meeting these needs. This manual is designed to provide assistance to the library manager who wants to offer ongoing in-house staff development. The models that are provided are designed to serve as resources for the managers who understand the necessity of becoming proficient in the art of training as well as in the art of selecting and directing others to become trainers for their institutions.

Chapters 1 and 2 will help the library director address the organization of a staff development program; Chapters 3 and 4 will focus on the importance of using skills which are already in place among staff members. Actual programs, curricula, handouts, and checklists are provided in Chapters 5 through 7. Chapter 8 will provide an overview of how to evaluate employees and how to evaluate the progress of the staff development program. Chapter 9 provides some ways of providing recognition for staff accomplishments, and Chapter 10 will put you in touch with resources that can assist you in developing your program.

Continuing opportunities for training are a necessity for every library if employees are to be able to achieve a uniform standard of performance. We want every patron to receive the same quality of service whether he or she is there at ten o'clock on Monday morning or at three o'clock on Saturday afternoon. We want our staff to be aware of and competent in the ways to deliver services that meet current patron needs, which may be a combination of new and traditional ones. The libraries we walk into today are quite different from the ones we may have known as children, or indeed from the ones that operated while we were in college. The past twenty years have brought such incredible changes in how we deliver library service and in the composition of the public to whom we deliver it that there is no doubt that we all frequently need refresher courses. Each of us must make a professional commitment to reach beyond our own library's walls through professional reading, workshops, and conferences. We cannot, however, stop there. The ongoing training that is the foundation of staff development is an additional piece of management responsibility that cannot be ignored.

Staff development must be concerned as well with the overall personal development of employees. The atmosphere which we try to create for patrons so that they will enjoy visiting us must equally be developed for the staff. It must be customer as well as worker friendly. We all spend a good portion of our lives in the workplace, so we should expect to be treated as well as those who are with us for only a few minutes of their day. This includes flexibility of scheduling, a comfortable area in which to take a break, safety and environmental precautions, and an overall concern for staff well-being. Staff will perform better if all members are treated with respect and dignity. This is the true foundation of staff development.

This book is intended to serve as a very practical guide for libraries which are interested in offering continuing staff training using a grass-roots approach. It contains many forms and handouts. You are invited to duplicate them as you need them, and to adopt them to your particular situation. It is hoped that this work will set your library on a course of continual self-improvement and that you can reflect that training through better service to your patrons.

1 WHAT THEY DIDN'T TEACH YOU IN LIBRARY SCHOOL

When we are fresh out of library school, clutching our shiny new MLSs, we are ready to tackle the world—or so we think. Our profession is changing so rapidly, however, that it doesn't take us long to realize that our training has limitations! For those of us who are a few years past commencement, the realization of the necessity of further learning to update skills and knowledge becomes increasingly stronger.

As a profession, we have been committed to the process of continuing education for many, many years. We have recognized that we need to build on our previously acquired knowledge, skills, and attitudes. We have attended workshops, seminars, and conferences faithfully in order to refresh our basic education, to master new concepts and methods, and to prepare for new areas of specialization. While this "out of the building" means of continued learning is valuable, and certainly appropriate in many cases, it should not be considered the one and only way of keeping ourselves and our staffs current.

Libraries are centers for lifelong learning. Through our services, we provide users with opportunities to continue their learning in ways that surpass the traditional boundaries of education. Why, then, have we consistently turned toward the traditional methods of education for our own development? Why do we not utilize our own skills in the provision of continuing education?

Workshops, seminars, and conferences are valid means of providing educational opportunities, and we should selectively choose those which can provide us with further development. The problem is that these require substantial registration fees and even travel, and in these times of dwindling budgets many of us can no longer find the financial resources to attend. The issue is compounded because we do not have enough staff to send some to workshops and have others cover their assigned tasks. We must find alternative ways to have all of our staff involved in continuing education, because the effective delivery of library services is dependent on competent library personnel. It is not an option to forgo the process on the excuse that we just don't have the money. Staff development is a more focused form of continuing professional education: focused on the particular need of staff in a given setting and on the mission of a particular library.

This book represents possible solutions to providing ongoing staff development to supplement the formal process. It is based on successful experiences. Because we depend on our staffs to perform productively, efficiently, and accurately, we believe we must have the assurance that they are always on the cutting edge. Our commitment to them is that we will provide the opportunities for them to update their knowledge and skills, as well as provide them with approaches to meet new challenges and to develop as individuals. Our hiring process includes a component of questioning to determine the prospective employees' attitudes toward this philosophy and their ideas of responsibility toward their own development. This being said, then, a good definition of *staff development* is the ongoing process that orients, trains, and develops, through a systematic approach, each member of a library organization to work together to serve its customers.

STAFF DEVELOPMENT DEFINED

Staff development includes a broad range of activities that address the developmental needs of both support and professional staff. These development activities can be position related or career related; they may address quality of work life or provide a means of personal enrichment. Their commonality is that they will help nurture a staff so that its members are more productive, more efficient, and more effective. Staff development differs from continuing education, as I have said, because it is geared to the specific needs of a particular institution. It can serve some of the same functions in that it can help staff attain knowledge and practice skills and reshape attitudes while becoming aware of current relevant trends. Yet it is different because it helps motivate, it keeps people from "burning out," and it helps them become aware of how their behavior affects the overall library operation.

In developing the mission and the goals of the library, the library administration must clearly realize that it does not exist in a vacuum. It is a major part of the management's responsibility to examine how the library fits into the overall community, how its goals correspond with goals of other organizations (such as Literacy Volunteers, United Way, Chamber of Commerce, etc.), and how the library can work with them cooperatively. The library's director has a responsibility to determine how its services can be part of the solution to society's problems. Public libraries do indeed have tremendous potential, and we are not living up to it. We need to broaden our vision of what public library services can mean to the community and what impact these services can have on the whole society. Consider, for instance, preschool programs. The youngsters who attend these programs develop language skills, social skills, and learn how to ask questions. They learn how to make the most of opportunities. These skills stay with them as they take part in other activities that life offers them. The impact makes a difference, and while the librarian who did a particular story hour may not realize it for years to come or ever, it may prove to be a significant example of how the library does indeed change lives. Our staffs need to be equipped with the best training possible in order to make this kind of impact and to be as broad thinking as possible about what library services could and should be.

A major point needs to be made about inclusiveness. Staff development must be offered to each and every staff member. In doing so, we recognize that it is the staff of the organization that makes it or breaks it. It is not the collection or the facility. Our product in libraries is service; our goal is excellent delivery of that service. The staff's performance in the workplace and its attitudes toward that workplace goes with all its members as they assume their other roles in the community. Ultimately, this is what will determine the overall success of the library. Although the director sets the direction of the library, the staff carries out the tasks to achieve that direction. Therefore, each and every staff member must be a good spokesperson for the library.

In order for the administrator to be comfortable with this process, and to share the authority of making the library's success, he or she will need to develop strong relationships with the staff. These relationships are built on mutual respect, but also on constancy, reliability, and integrity. This process will enhance both performance and attitude, because the staff will be empowered through consistent staff development.

As organizations, libraries have become more and more aware of the necessity of building goodwill within our communities. Thus we have found more and more libraries utilizing public relations programs. A cardinal rule of public relations in the business sector is that you must first establish a good product before you try to sell it. Libraries should follow this example and recognize that a thorough staff development program is what will motivate the people within your organization to become advocates for it.

INTERNAL MARKETING

The basis of building the good product is a solid internal marketing program. This simply is building goodwill, competence, and confidence internally so that the external result will follow naturally. There are several components to this internal marketing plan. The emphasis on these components will vary from library to library, but they are the critical foundation on which a staff development program will build. This also illustrates another significant difference between continuing education and staff development, and emphasizes the value of our grass-roots methods. Staff development programs must be personalized if they are going to meet the needs of a particular staff and administration in a particular library within a specific time frame. I hope that you will consider what I have written from my experience, as an example of the process and adapt its programs and ideas rather than duplicate them. This adaptation process is key if your staff development program is to become personalized enough to fit your unique library, staff, and situation.

Personal contacts are the number one method of developing an internal marketing plan and of beginning the process of personalizing the workplace. Absolutely nothing will work better for a manager than knowing his or her employees as people. Through sincere concern and understanding of employees' needs, a manager will begin to develop a relationship with the staff. From efforts to implement changes to meet these needs will result a building of loyalty to the organization.

People want to be recognized as valuable to an organization, and they want to know that they have made contributions to it and are in fact shareholders in its success. Most people adopt the behavior of those around them, so it is definitely beneficial for the administrators to exhibit behavior that they would like to see duplicated. This becomes especially important in larger organizations because the CEOs must then depend on middle management to carry out much of the relationship-building process on their behalf.

Internal marketing will set the stage for your staff development program if you invest some time in planning your approach thoroughly, and if you follow that plan consistently. This will link the employees to the organization's mission and create a sense of pride and achievement for all. A sense of ownership results when employees have been encouraged to be creative and contribute ideas, when their input has been valued, and when feedback has been provided. Employees must know what the mission is and be enthusiastic about supporting it.

All managers in every type of library want to have customer-friendly organizations. We all want to project a positive image to our users, and we devote time and resources to publicity campaigns (including brochures, logos, bookmarks, etc.) in order to achieve this. Far too few of us, however, realize that in order for the library to have a favorable image in the community, we must first be able to project this positiveness internally, so we must invest both our time and our efforts into building the carriers with which our libraries project this positiveness—*our staffs*. Libraries are by nature service organizations. Their value should not be measured by the number of items they hold, but rather by the number of successful user transactions. These transactions are what are facilitated by our staffs, and it is the staff that delivers the service. *People*, not things, are what make or break an organization. It is therefore reasonable to expect that we develop thorough, organized internal marketing programs before we go to great lengths to publicize our library services externally.

Our employees are our image. They are our best, and unfortunately in some cases our worst, advertisements. The library's internal marketing program is necessary for communicating purposes, but even more importantly for the commitment and the pride that staff members develop for their organization when they have a thorough understanding of what their library is all about. They need to be aware of its mission, they must become believers in it, and then they are likely to become spokespersons for it. Internal marketing makes employees feel valued. The result is that the library becomes a nicer place to work and a nicer place to visit.

In order for an internal marketing program to be effective, the staff members must realize that they are part of an organization that is doing good things. Positive actions influence others more than any number of words, and people will reciprocate with positive actions of their own. For employees to make a commitment to action, they must be convinced that they are working for a good cause. They are then able to visualize what library service could be. They can develop this vision if they are participants in developing not only the library's goals but also the plan of action necessary to reach those goals. This is the essence of people power, which comes from the administration's sharing its authority with individuals they have come to value for their constancy, their reliability, and their integrity. Internal marketing is about developing this mutual respect.

Internal marketing has results when it is approached by an administration in a manner that demonstrates its pride in the organization and in its commitment to excellence. Not all methods will be appropriate for all locations or all situations, but for the purposes of a definition, *internal marketing* is the infiltration of the organization's mission into all aspects of its function. Internal marketing is training, both through orientation to the particular organization and through long-term professional development. Internal marketing is communications, both oral and written. My guess is that if any of us surveyed our staffs they would tell us that the main way that they get information about the organization is through the grapevine. We all know how information changes when it comes secondhand or, worse yet, through three or more people. If we ask our employees how they would *prefer* to hear important information, however, the grapevine would rank as their least favorite method. Employees want to be valued and trusted, so they want to receive information from their supervisors, their personal connection with authority. Depending on the importance of the information, employees like to receive newsletters or memos as well. These methods help overcome the inevitable "who knew first" and "nobody told me" syndromes, and again create a sense of belonging.

In a later chapter, thematic programs will be presented as models in staff development, one of which is a communications program. So often we undervalue this basic human need and fail to recognize that a weak input and feedback system is detrimental to an organization. Every organization has its grapevine through which to disseminate information, but as in that old-fashioned children's game of Telephone, as the information travels from one to another on the grapevine, it is changed—maybe for lack of understanding, or to shorten the story, or it may change as individual emotions come into play. Internal marketing cannot depend on the grapevine method if it is to reach everyone with the same message; rather a combined system of information dissemination should be in place. We should be rather good at this since it is central to our profession! Personal contacts, small group meetings, a bulletin board, or an employee newsletter will all be useful in developing a strong communications network for internal marketing.

In addition to communications, staff members must be helped to identify with your organization. Attractive name badges and business cards help establish this identity. Personal contacts are strengthened through recognition of special events in a person's life (birthday, anniversary) or the achievements of family members, genuine assistance during times of need, and social opportunities which bring the staff together to celebrate, to relax, and even to share sorrow.

Employee recognition programs are another part of internal marketing. If we want employees to strive for excellence, we must set the standards for that excellence. We must praise their achievements and contributions, and ensure that these individuals are appreciated by their colleagues and the decision-makers alike. Include the recognition in a newspaper, share it at a staff meeting, hold celebrations. Monetary remuneration is important, but we should not overlook the human satisfaction employees get when we commend them on a job well done.

The administration participates in internal marketing when it exhibits care through the personal environment that is provided for the staff. While work areas do not need to be luxurious, they should be clean, safe, comfortable, and reasonably attractive. In turn, concern about employees influences how they feel about their organization.

An administrator who wants to have a successful organization is wise to develop an internal marketing program that will allow for the integration of attitude and efforts. This process will contribute to the achievement of the library's goals. Our responsibility is to make organizations the very best they can be. To do so, I believe that we must put our employees first. Then our patrons will receive a level of service that comes from the heart, and they will be able to appreciate its value even more.

ADULT LEARNERS

A word should be said about the adult learning process, which is significantly different than the learning process of childhood. Adults bring to their workplace and to workshops an established set of skills, a body of knowledge, and certain attitudes about work and education which can affect the outcome of the process. People learn through a variety of methods; there is no one right way! Orientation, staff meetings, readings of professional materials, workshops, lectures, and formal course work are some of the options to be explored. The trainer should consider some variation of method within their work as well—from the use of audiovisual materials for visual learners to role-playing, brainstorming, and other participatory activities for others.

Adults have to be able to see the impact of learning on job

performance in order to put themselves in the proper frame of mind to learn. In order to maximize motivation for adults, the participants must be made to believe that the materials covered will increase their effectiveness, add to their professional skills, and enhance the skills they already have. Job satisfaction is realized in people who have an investment in their training; this consideration helps create a good psychological foundation for the entire learning process.

If these simple yet critical steps are taken, your organization will be a pleasure to work in. If you set up a consistent plan to oversee staff development, you will be on your way to creating an organizational culture to meet your mission of providing excellent library service to the community, which will catch on to the attitudes as well as the resources and services you are providing and will repay you handsomely with its loyal support.

2 BEGINNING A STAFF DEVELOPMENT PROGRAM IN YOUR LIBRARY

Libraries, by their very nature, are labor intensive organizations. While we depend upon our resources, it is even more important to have a staff that is able to perform the most essential function: matching the information resources to the needs of the individual user. A staff that is able to do this must be highly productive and well motivated. The process that will result in development of this type of staff clearly starts by hiring the right person for the job. Your overall plan for staff development begins with the job description you release for advertisement, continues through the interview phase, is heightened during the orientation and training introduction to your library, and then is updated and supported through day-to-day activity.

PLANNING FOR STAFF DEVELOPMENT

This overall plan for staff development is the most crucial element in determining if you will be able to have an organized, purposeful program in place. It is an investment of time that will have tremendous payoff. The planning process helps determine the long-term vision of the library, and it helps identify ways to fulfill the goals. The staff development program at your library should be in a continuous, closed-loop that perpetuates a healthy, growing entity. Not only will there be fewer problems in a workplace that has a built-in nurturing system, but the employees will be better able to relate their everyday work tasks to the underlying goals and objectives of the library.

There are some essential decisions that the library's management will have to make before the planning process for staff development begins. First and foremost, the library should be sure that its program is visionary—you want to prepare for the future, but at the same time the program must remain realistic in terms of present needs, and it must be achievable. The program should be flexible enough to encompass new ideas and to be able to explore new developments and trends, but it should establish the library's direction for growth and services clearly and specifically. The staff development program must provide a living framework of support, a framework that is capable of adaptation. Ultimately, it must relate closely to the library's goals and objectives. To do this, it must be driven by those priorities which reflect the users' needs. The planning process provides the time to think about how to balance the knowledge that you have about past performance with the realities of the present and the opportunities for the future.

This type of overall plan for staff development will result in a more organized and a more comprehensive program. It will provide all of the staff members with a broader perspective on the library as a whole as well as showing how their particular positions fit into the whole scheme of service.

This planning begins with the identification of specific issues and training needs within the library. A needs-assessment process, very similar to the ones that we do concerning our library services to the community, is necessary in order to develop programs that will be truly responsive to the needs of both the organization and the employees. You will want to discover what the employees think they need. You must also determine what the organization thinks the employees need to know in order to have a successful library. Some samples of helpful tools for this process are presented at the end of the chapter.

This needs-assessment process leads right into the next step of the program: defining the learning objectives, which will be used to establish a list of what skills must be learned in a particular workshop so that participants know what to expect. There are several reasons that these objectives need to be laid out at the beginning of the program. First of all, you will have a way to measure results since you will be able to compare post-workshop skills with entry-level skills. Second, the presenter or trainer will have a clear understanding of what is expected in each session. All participants should be presented with these objectives in written form at the start of the series. This will help underline the objectives, and alert participants to what the administration expects of them. These learning objectives do not necessarily summarize the program, but sharing them sets the tone and facilitates learning. Content of the workshop will be shaped to meet these learning objectives and should be determined with the presenters or trainer.

Chapter 3 will provide assistance in reaching these decisions with the trainer. For planning purposes, however, it is important to consider the following factors in determining who will be the trainer for any given workshop. First of all, you must take into consideration what results you want. Then, your next step will be to determine which methods of training to use. You can have a program with terrific content, but if the learning methods are not appropriate to a particular audience, learning will not take place. Time, group size, and environmental considerations must all be part of the information used to develop the program design. The expertise and reputation of the trainer will assist you with this.

The program design is what will ultimately determine learning success, since this is the vehicle for the delivery of the message that you want your staff to receive. It will be structured consistently through the progression of the workshop so that the learning objectives will be achieved. In order for this to happen, a program must be implemented for the right reasons, using the learning methods that will hold the participants' interest while involving them in the learning process. It must be clearly related to participant and institutional needs.

Successful learning is accomplished when the participants are able to relate new materials to a familiar context. It is easier to comprehend something if the learning is intended to be an expansion of a preexisting knowledge base. If the topic is a totally new one, then the training designs will have to present a truly coherent overview of the materials and then relate the presentation to past experiences as often as possible. It will also be necessary to project how the new skills will improve job performance.

PRACTICE NEW SKILLS TO REINFORCE THEM

The opportunity to practice newly acquired skills provides the repetition and reinforcement that some individuals need to complete their learning as well as being a way for the trainer to evaluate the progress of the participant's skills. This practice reinforces the objectives because the on-the-job application of skills illustrates the importance of these objectives. This practice in many instances feeds back components of the training, which provides a way to observe and measure the outcome. The library management is especially interested in the changes in attitudes and the actual attainment of knowledge of the staff. Decisions can then be made to alter the training or to add additional training to the program.

The following points are significant in the adult learning process and should be remembered in designing the program:

- Adults have less time to participate in learning because of their many responsibilities. The time spent in training sessions must be viewed as a worthwhile investment if they are going to participate.
- The pressures of normal day-to-day tasks limit the attention span of adults. This affects the time of day when you should offer programs as well as the length of the sessions.
- The trainer selected is not viewed as an authority figure, but as a resource person. The attitude of the trainer must reflect this.
- Adults do not always view themselves as learners or as needing to learn, most often because of the responsibilities they already carry. They must be convinced that we all learn from one another.
- Most of our work involves repetitive situations. Planning an exciting, creative way to expand job horizons brings a welcome change to routine when accepted and integrated into the worker's own style.
- People do things for their own reasons! Motivation to learn cannot be pressed onto employees. Rather, it comes when the participants are offered learning situations that are relevant to them.

Your organization has an obligation to offer learning opportunities; however, an individual must assume responsibility for his or her own development. Administrators who display an enthusiastic willingness to learn help this process immeasurably.

An effective staff development program is the result of careful planning, and the decision to share the responsibility with the participants indicates that they, too, are an integral part of the planning process. The following pages will provide the staff development coordinator at your library with a set of models that can be used to gather the information needed to begin to plan for staff development at your library. A word of caution is necessary here: Please remember to adapt the forms to your own particular library. This is critically important because only with a personalized method of collecting data will you have a personalized program that is suited to your needs. In the following chapters, samples will be provided for the other components of the plan.

METHODS TO DETERMINE TRAINING NEEDS

Training needs can be determined by finding what is presently being done by each staff member and matching that information with what could or should be done, and establishing priorities. The gap between these two factors will provide you with clues as to the type and the amount of training that is needed within your library. This assessment can be accomplished by using a combination of techniques. It is important to understand that no one method alone will provide all the information necessary to determine the training needs for the library. At the end of this chapter, as well as at the end of the following chapters, there are a series of worksheets. These should be used by the library director to implement a staff development program. These examples were designed to provide a step-by-step guide for the establishment of the program: 1. its inception, including determining the needs of the particular library; 2. implementing the program; and 3. evaluating its success.

WRITTEN SOURCES

Survey: The survey method is an excellent way to determine what your library is or is not doing. This should be accomplished in the form of a printed questionnaire consisting of a list of questions. In some cases, the same form is good for everyone. In others, managers may need to use one and front-line staff another. In any case, the questions should be brief, specific, and phrased in a way that demands a short answer. It is a good idea to conduct a survey at least twice a year. In this way, the surveys will point out improvements that have occurred as the result of training and will uncover any new training needs. The speed with which our profession has been changing dictates a need for frequent re-assessment.

Letters (memos, suggestions, etc.) of request and complaint should be taken seriously. This is a great source to determine training needs. Read between the lines; many times what the writer of the note is complaining about is not the entire need, but the symptom of another problem.

Meeting minutes, logs, newsletters, etc., from different departments may be sources of information. Read them thoroughly to determine the attitudes that they convey.

Plans of action: Are there formal, written goals and objectives for different departments? How well are objectives being met? These plans may give you a good idea of some of the supportive training the staff will need in order to carry out projected activities.

UNWRITTEN SOURCES

Informal talks: You can have these talks in any setting. Consider what you hear in the coffee break area, the hallways, and the parking lot. There are valuable clues around, and you may need to listen between the lines as well to casual comments about personalities and situations.

Observations: Become a subscriber to the "walk around" school of management. An alert and creative mind, with good eyes and a discreet mouth, are valuable in collecting this data. When you get back to your desk, write down key observations so that you will not forget them.

Interviews: Formal one-to-one meetings or small group meetings are excellent ways to assess learning needs. Be prepared for these. Write down a few questions that require more than a yes or no answer. Write the answers down. Be prepared to listen as well as to ask questions because you are *indeed* listening for people to tell you what they think they need or want.

PROGRAM PLAN

To implement a good staff development program, the library director should follow a complete and thorough process to be sure that nothing has been overlooked. This process begins with developing the needs of the particular institution through a series of formal and informal assessment tools. The manager must clearly understand and state in writing what the purpose of the training is. This must be clear to the trainer and to the staff that will be trained. The next step will be selecting the right trainer for the program. It may be someone on the staff who has the experience that you want shared with other employees, or it may be an outside person. In either case, the library director and the trainer must have an agreement or contract which specifically states what is expected of each party. This agreement should take into consideration the training methods as well as the overall program design. The library director must make a commitment that goes beyond the training process to the application of the newly learned skills. Appropriate and sufficient time to apply these skills must be planned for and then supervised. Last, but certainly not least, is the function of evaluation. This closes the loop and gives the library director the opportunity to see if the learning has taken hold and is being used or if further or different training opportunities should be considered. Figure 2.1 summarizes these concepts.

Figure 2.1 Program Plan: Staff Development/The Process

Needs Assessment
Learning Objectives
Contracting
Methods
Design
Application of Learning
Evaluation
Environmental Impacts
Global
National
State/Province
Library
What is happening that will have implications
for the library and how it delivers service?

Keeping this overview in mind will lead you through the process of planning a staff development program. Before you can proceed, the management of the library must be able to articulate the mission of the library, and ensure that it is communicated to others.

Figure 2.2 Needs Assessment: Leader Audit for Management

Yes No

___ ___ Does the library have a clear, well-written, concise statement of goals and objectives?

___ ___ Are you authoritative, decisive, and firm?

___ ___ Do you seek ideas and suggestions from the rest of the staff?

___ ___ Do you enforce rules and decisions fairly for everyone?

___ ___ Do you allocate scarce resources according to predetermined priorities?

___ ___ Do you spend at least half of your time interacting with staff and community?

___ ___ Does your collection include resources for all segments of the community?

___ ___ Do you encourage training opportunities to improve the performance of your staff?

___ ___ Are you enthusiastic about library services and express your reasons for your sense of purpose?

___ ___ Are you committed to being on the cutting edge of informational services?

___ ___ Have you distributed statements of expectations and standards for staff performance?

___ ___ Do YOU meet these expectations and standards?

___ ___ Is there a coherent, consistent plan for regular assessment of all staff?

___ ___ Do you share these experiences with supporters (trustees, friends)?

___ ___ Do you keep your governing officials and general public informed about staff training?

___ ___ Do you relate the training to new or improved services so the user can appreciate the importance of these training opportunities?

Figure 2.3 Needs Assessment: Training Needs Identification

Think back over the last six to twelve months in your library. Try to recall incidents which were handled either very well or very poorly. Then complete the following:

Briefly describe the incident.

What were the negative or positive consequences of the incident?

What factors led to it or contributed to it?

On the basis of your analysis of the incident, what type of training might have prevented or lessened the negative consequences or contributed to the positive consequences?

Both managers and front-line staff should complete this form.

Figure 2.4 Needs Assessment: Training Needs Survey

Job Title or Department _____

Please review the items carefully. Consider each in relation to your work and the extent to which you feel adequately trained to perform it. Please rate as follows: 1. does not apply; 2. important; 3. essential.

	Importance of my work	Need for more training
1. Knowledge of philosophy, politics, and procedures		
2. Information about the library collection		
3. Information about the library building, including space utilization		
4. Time management		
5. How to use statistics		
6. How to analyze user needs		
7. How to conduct a reference interview		
8. Patron confidentiality		
9. Oral and written communication skills		
10. How to deal with difficult people		

Figure 2.5 Seminar Purposes

As a result of this seminar, participants will:
1. understand the role and the importance of internal marketing in achieving excellence in programs and institutions;
2. understand their role as catalysts in staff development with reference to their own institution;
3. recognize that they and many others of the staff already have the skills necessary to implement a successful staff development program; and
4. become aware of techniques used in business that can be successfully adapted and applied to library staffs.

3 DEVELOPING INDIVIDUAL POTENTIAL IN YOUR LIBRARY

The staff's involvement in the library's staff development program begins during the needs assessment process discussed in Chapter 2. This critical step is required for the staff to develop a sense of commitment to the process. As a manager, you may find useful some reinforcement techniques for keeping the employees involved and interested. First and foremost will be the sense of achievement employees feel when they are able to apply the knowledge or skill acquired from participation in a staff development program. Two other ways of providing this reinforcement will be discussed more thoroughly in later chapters but bear mentioning here: 1. using staff members as trainers, and 2. finding ways, in addition to salary increases, to recognize and reward performance. In any case, a sense of achievement is most often what will provide the motivation for individuals to continue their participation, because by its very nature motivation is an internal, personal response. It cannot be provided solely by an outside influence.

WHO IS IN CHARGE OF STAFF DEVELOPMENT?

Many large companies and even some libraries have a staff member whose position (as, for example, human resources director) includes the responsibility of overseeing staff development within the organization. Most libraries, however, are not able to afford such a position, so the responsibility falls upon the shoulders of someone else in the organization. If this is indeed the case, the library administration must state emphatically that staff development is a priority, or it will become lost among the myriad other tasks this individual has. I have found that this responsibility has gone to the assistant director or to department managers. Each library will have to determine what staffing configuration is the right one for its particular situation. In any case, the duties would be very similar. The staff development coordinator will find it necessary to follow the planning process, discussed in Chapter 2, from the needs assessment right on through the feedback and evaluation components. In addition, duties would include deciding whether to use an outside trainer or someone on the staff who has both expertise in a given area *and* the ability to train. The person in charge must be able to articulate the learning objectives to the trainer and to the staff. In some situation, it might also be necessary for the development coordinator to convince authorities of the necessity for investing time, money, and effort in the training, and might even spearhead a fund-raising campaign in order to cover staff development expenses.

HOW MUCH WILL IT COST?

There is no hard-and-fast rule about the amount of time or money that should be allocated to a staff development program. It will vary from library to library. It is true that the programs can cost no additional money, or they can cost hundreds of dollars, but we must recognize that there is always some cost involved—the staff time invested is an example. If you invite an outside speaker and must pay an honorarium or travel expenses; if you purchase books or videos; if you make copies—all of these things will cost money. Remember also to factor in the time needed to implement the changes and to follow up with feedback. Your budget may already have a line for conferences and meetings. Add a subdivision to it, and include your ongoing staff training.

The following is a way to estimate the cost that your agency will be committing in time, if not in actual dollars, to a staff development program. As you look at this chart, I would like you to remember that these costs are estimates. You will need to plug in the actual amount per hour for your staff. Remember as you estimate that the cost of *not* having ongoing staff training will, in the long run, far surpass these estimates.

Sample Budget: Training Needs Assessment	
Hours	*Cost*
10 by staff development coordinator	$150–200
2 by # of librarians	$200–300
2 by # of paraprofessionals	$150–250
Planning by staff development coordinator	
5 hours	$100

Sample Budget Continued	
Hours	*Cost*
Program design by trainer (on staff), or the hiring of trainer 5 hours	$100
Training program experience 2 hours by all staff	$400–500
Practice 20 hours by all staff	$4,000–5,000
Evaluation 1 hour by trainer 10 hours by supervisors	$50 $200–400

HONORARIA FOR OUTSIDE TRAINERS

If you are very fortunate, there will be local individuals in businesses or other organizations who will come to your agency for a minimal cost. A nice thank you of a gift certificate is usually appropriate. If you expect people to take the time from their schedules to do presentations for you, however, you should be prepared to pay travel and food expenses as well as an honorarium. These honoraria can range from twenty-five on up to thousands of dollars. Be prepared! Choose carefully and remember that the most touted "big name" in trainers might not be best for your precise training niche even if you could afford them.

MOTIVATION OF STAFF TO PARTICIPATE

There are two primary times within the motivation cycle that the staff development coordinator can exert some influence: during the involvement and reinforcement phases. It is at these points in the process when the library, not the individual, is in control. In effect, this is what makes staff development a good example of a partnership. The library has an obligation to offer learning experiences and a responsibility to reward improved performance. Individual employees have the responsibility of doing more than showing up. They must decide to commit themselves to the achievement of greater competency levels. This motivation toward the pursuit of excellence then rests entirely within each employee's control, though of course in extreme cases the library management always has the option of dissatisfaction with performance and whatever follows.

From the library's perspective, then, the staff development program must maximize itself in the areas where it has positive control. It is not good enough just to have a training program. The library must be prepared to offer *excellent* training if it wants to have excellently prepared employees. In order to do this effectively, the person who is in charge of developing the programs must have a thorough understanding of the principles of adult learning and motivation. Having this type of information provides trainers with the background needed to provide that excellent training opportunity. It will help them organize their materials, and it will determine the presentation style they will use in their training. It is in this way that the trainer will be able to assist the participants in making the most of their natural abilities.

LEARNING TECHNIQUES

These are some basic techniques that are recognized as being appropriate for adult learning. The first point to consider is that the trainer should be prepared to keep the participants active during the workshop. Adults do not have a high tolerance for sitting and listening. This is why it is so important to establish an active atmosphere, providing opportunities for both input and response during the training period. If there is a lecture portion of the session, a good strategy to remember is to pause after each major idea is presented. Asking the participants how this idea or concept might affect their particular jobs is a way to clarify as well as to involve the participants. Second, adult participants are better able to understand new ideas if examples are provided. This will assist the participants in incorporating the knowledge presented into their own knowledge base and applying it to their work. Role-playing or practice of a skill in a simulated situation helps to involve participants and reinforce the ideas presented.

From these techniques, you can see that the trainer is maximizing the involvement factor in order to keep the participants focused on the program. *Learning is an act of change, and in most cases adults resist change.* This causes them to challenge their need for further learning. The trainer can help them minimize their resistance by providing them with positive feedback. Helping participants understand the meaning of their new knowledge and helping them relate their newly learned skills to real life and already familiar experiences can also be accomplished through question-and-answer sessions. In any event, the material presented to adult learners should be directed toward immediate application. When the information provided applies immediately to one's experiences or background, understanding is increased. The old standby test is, Is it relevant? Starting with familiar ideas and concepts creates an environment of relevance and makes participants more receptive to absorbing and integrating new information. All of these strategies will help the library plan a more effective staff development program, because the program design is intended to maximize adult learning.

In addition to adult learning processes, the staff development plan of the library will require the use of a variety of methods and techniques that lend themselves to the scope of the concepts that might be presented. Having a repertoire of these to choose from will also serve to keep the programs exciting and fresh.

Starting with an **icebreaker** is especially helpful if there are many new people in the group. This technique is a way to introduce people to one another in a manner that is relaxed and minimizes self-consciousness. A common icebreaker is to pair people and have them share information with each other for three to five minutes. At the end of the allotted time, the partner shares the information that he or she learned about the new colleague. This had the benefit of introducing people to one another, but it also sets a relaxed tone for the session and allows for some boasting that one would not do for oneself.

Discussion is an important part of both large and small training sessions. It is a very useful technique since so much of our training needs revolve around issues. Small group **breakouts** and **brainstorming sessions** are specific examples of the discussion techniques. These methods are especially useful when the library management is interested in having the group formulate a solution to a particular problem. In this type of training session, the trainer in actuality becomes a facilitator. The question or cues the facilitator gives should be geared to eliciting ideas from all of the participants. The group should not criticize or dispose of ideas during the process. They should instead wait until all of the ideas are presented, and then evaluate each of them in terms of its practicality as part of the solution. Having the staff evaluate alternative solutions and choose the one that the majority feels is most suitable is a gigantic step toward solving the problem. The group can then move on to determine what other steps are needed to achieve the desired result and with the facilitator's assistance assign responsibilities to its members for moving the process forward.

The library, if it chooses to use this form of training, must clearly spell out what result will be expected. Management must guarantee the participants in this group process the freedom to implement their plan. The trainer or facilitator should not give his or her own viewpoint, because doing so will have the effect of telling the participants what they should do. The trainer's job is to listen to the discussion and see that the participants do not lose sight of their purpose. The trainer should also assist the group in summarizing their plans so that they can then be implemented.

In some instances, especially when the participants have not had problem-solving experience, it is very useful to employ case studies. Like examples, case studies often have the effect of making the learning situation more relevant to the participant, rather than dealing with broad issues or concepts. A case study is actually a written description of a given situation. It teaches how to analyze important aspects and how to arrive at conclusions or solutions. In many situations, when interpersonal relationships are at stake, this method will help the staff develop insight. Participants will learn how to separate the relevant facts from those which are not important. Most crucial of all, the participants will learn through this method that if they communicate with one another, they will be able to see matters from more than one point of view and therefore will be more flexible in the workplace. Case studies are one of my favorite methods of training, because regardless of the content or the intended outcome, the most important lesson of all—**communicating**—is learned.

I would be remiss if I did not mention that old standby of learning: the **lecture** method. The lecture is an informative presentation, designed to explain an idea or a concept, by the trainer, who has much more knowledge of the subject than the group to be trained. If the group has some basic knowledge of the subject, it would be much better to use one of the above-mentioned training strategies instead. Lectures can be direct, clear presentations of the facts in a relatively short time frame. If the trainer is not a good speaker or is not well prepared, however, the lecture method can become dull and deadly. My advice would be to use this method sparingly—choosing a trainer who is always well organized, well prepared, and able to deliver the material in an interesting way. The right person in the right situation can inspire a group and motivate desire to learn and to do.

SELECTING TRAINERS

In order to design a staff development program that will bring out the best in your staff, the library must have a clear idea of its training philosophy and select trainers whose styles are in tune with it. What the library administration perceives to be important is what will guide the design of the training program. The approach that the trainer takes will also rest on this, and it will require a professional attitude, credibility, and organizational skills. The program design will include a statement known as the training or learning objective, which will describe the intended result. This is the performance standard that you want your staff to exhibit in the workplace at the conclusion of the training. The development and statement of the objective will help the trainer develop the necessary materials for the workshop, decide what method of presentation to use, and design a method of evaluation so that the library will be able to determine if the training was successful.

In designing a program, there are several factors to consider that may influence the outcome. The person organizing the staff development program for the library must be in the position of knowing the capabilities of the group. What its members will be capable of learning in a given period should be clear. The planner must consider time factors: How much time can the library spend on any given program and on the staff development during a given year? The amount of time allotted is directly tied into the result. The library must weigh the expense (time is money) against the anticipated benefits that the library will receive as a result of the training. Is the result worth it? Other cost factors to consider in addition to time are printing for handouts, perhaps a manual, and refreshments.

After receiving overall directions from the staff development coordinator, the trainer has the responsibility to determine the material that will be covered in the session(s); the length of time necessary to teach the material; to develop any handouts or bibliographies that will be used during the program; and to determine which training methods will be most effective in the given situation. Many of the examples that are provided at the end of the chapters can be used as they appear, or they can serve as examples of the kinds of handouts that participants like to have.

The trainer takes on the responsibility of developing or gathering together the course materials if the library has clearly indicated its expectations. In any event, two types of resource materials should be included in developing the content of training sessions.

Naturally, most of the materials utilized are specially designed with librarians in mind. This helps make learning situations appropriate to the particular staff members. We must remember, however, that we should use external resources as well. These materials are not strictly related to libraries, but that is actually their greatest value. Borrowing proven techniques and strategies from other organizations prevents us from constantly reinventing the wheel. In addition to being an incredible time saver, this is a wonderful way of integrating libraries into the mainstream and of bringing useful methods and concepts from the mainstream into library thinking. Other agencies will begin to recognize the similarities of our organizations' needs with their own and will have a better understanding of our missions.

The framework for the training program is developed in the program outline, which includes the learning objectives. The broad context area of this objective proceeds in the outline from simple to more complex concepts. This will help you progress through the program in an organized fashion.

Because there are so many needs to address, the trainer will need to use as many methods as possible to create an environment conducive to adult learning. The physical setting of the program, as well as other courtesies (e.g., having coffee available) should be considered in the program designing phase. Enhancement of learning takes place when the participants are comfortable and satisfied. Air quality, temperature, and seating arrangements are all a part of the overall picture.

Creating a sense of continuity within a training session is also important. This can be accomplished be repetition of the salient points throughout the program so that they are reinforced. Each time one of these points is repeated, more information can be given so that comprehension is growing sequentially. Substantive presentations can also be enlivened with humor and with interesting language. While we do not intend to present a show, we want people to enjoy learning. A small shot of humor often serves to make a point memorable.

There is no question that if you intend to develop individual potential within your library, you must influence the thinking of your group and perhaps even sell them on a particular idea, point of view, or attitude. That is the purpose that you are trying to achieve. So, without a doubt, the following minimums must be met by the training design and by the selection of a trainer in order for the library to achieve its purpose. Presenters must be knowledgeable. The better prepared they are, the more they are able to instill a sense of confidence in the group. Confidence comes only when there is knowledge. It is important for presenters to be themselves; being natural helps make you most effective. Never pretend to know an answer when you don't. Honesty is better, and people will respect you more if you admit that you don't know but you are willing to find out and get back to them.

The manner of presentation is critically important in determining the overall success of the staff development program, so the organizer should be prepared to exhibit desirable traits or find presenters who are able to be comfortable as well as knowledgeable in providing training. Attributes of effective trainers include the ability to be tactful, calm, and open-minded. They should also be authoritative enough to inspire confidence, trust, and respect. Good trainers are able to be objective, adaptable to a variety of situations, and enthusiastic. They are able to cope with the unexpected and even turn a difficult situation to good use. The training process is one of teaching and communication, so it is important to create a good psychological foundation for it. The trainer must be ready to control the process to provide the broadest possible perspective on the course materials.

We often assume that staff development occurs only in formal learning situations. This is a rather limited view. Many everyday situations lend themselves to effective teaching and learning. A casual discussion with one of your staff members can provide an opportunity to reinforce a certain organizational value, clarify a question about a particular assignment, or suggest a specific resource that may be helpful. A library that is geared up to provide ongoing staff development will take advantage of these situations as they arise. This can even be extended to the assignment of tasks. Rather than have the same people complete particular tasks all the time, having new people do it will provide an opportunity for growth. This is the same with delegation. Rather than do tasks yourself, ask others to do them for you, so that they too learn how to perform the tasks. As the manager, it is your responsibility to provide feedback on these assignments as they progress, not just during a performance review. Feedback needs to be provided in a specific, timely, and constructive manner. This is an integral part of the manager's job.

The library director or staff development coordinator needs to make a personal commitment to each employee who is going to realize potential within your organization. Finding out about employees' interests, their values, and their aspirations, as well as finding out the particular areas in which they want to improve, will set the pace for the development program. It is a measure of the successful leadership of the organization that the individuals for whom leaders are responsible are becoming accomplished.

WHAT TO LOOK FOR IN A TRAINER

While no one person will embody all of the following characteristics, this is a good checklist of some of the character traits and abilities of trainers that result in good training programs.

- Good trainers are task oriented. They are able to accept responsibility, and they are adaptable to change.
- Good trainers are able to challenge people in their teaching by making them stretch to achieve the best of which they are capable. The best trainers are expert in their field, and they are able to relate to other subject areas. Good trainers are up to date in all areas of their profession. They take refresher courses, attend conferences and professional meetings, keep up with professional literature, and are willing to try new methods. They are credible because they know what they are talking about.
- Good trainers keep their cool in difficult circumstances. They are patient and interested in their students' needs. They relate to the participants as individuals and listen to their ideas.
- Good trainers use a variety of teaching methods and techniques to help students learn quickly and effectively. They will adapt their teaching methods to what the students need to learn.
- Good trainers are enthusiastic, firm yet fair, able to admit that they are wrong, and have a good sense of humor. They have a keen understanding of self. In order to help others, trainers must first understand their own strengths and weaknesses, likes and dislikes.

Figure 3.1 Trainer Checklist

	Yes	No
1. Has a grasp of the staff's present knowledge and skills		
2. Knows what knowledge and skills will be required to achieve the library's vision and complete the terms of its present mission		
3. Views staff development as a primary job function		
4. Has a strategy for developing needed knowledge and skills		
5. Gets satisfaction from helping others develop		
6. Is able to diagnose performance problems		
7. Takes an open-minded approach to dealing with problems		
8. Takes mistakes in stride as long as individuals learn from them		
9. Is sincere and honest, not critical, in giving feedback		
10. Promotes lifelong learning and demonstrates it for the staff		

Following is a basic outline in a standard format that should prove to be very useful for the trainer. It is designed to prompt one to think about who the audience is, how long the program should be in relation to the audience and the subject, and to keep in mind what the intended results of the training (the learning objectives) are supposed to be. As the trainer develops his or her presentation, this will provide the guide for considering how the material is going to be delivered, what resource materials to use, etc.

Figure 3.2   Sample Training Outline

Training Topic (List the subject):

Training Target (Who are you training? How many people?):

Training Time (Length of the program):

Training Objectives (What is the intended result?):

I.   Broad Content Area

    A. First subdivision

        1. Subheading

            a. topic

            b. topic

        2. Subheading

            a. topic

            b. topic

Training Technique (What method will you use?):

Training Aids (What will you use? Audiovisuals, etc. ?):

Training Setup (What will room setup be? Hint: round tables facilitate face to face discussion):

Other Needs:

4 EDUCATING ONE ANOTHER

Central to the policies that guide any organization are the issues that relate to human resources. We should be investing a tremendous amount of effort into human resources because people are the prime component of any service organization. The question that often arises is, How can this be accomplished with the limited resources that libraries and most other nonprofit organizations have at their disposal? One of the best solutions that I know is to take advantage of the very talents that are possessed by the staff. These can be applied to the training program as required. In actuality, you have the opportunity to develop a network in which all members have a responsibility to succeed because they also have a stake in the organization's mission to develop human skills. Sharing the responsibility encourages the staff members to be creative and to move toward helping the library accomplish its goals—a motivation that will keep staff members focused.

In order to develop an effective network of staff trainers and support systems, the employees must have a sense of empowerment. Empower does not mean that the manager dumps all of the grunt work on the employees. Rather, it refers to the delegation of both authority and decision-making. The process of empowerment is dependent upon vision, upon resources, and upon the employees' ability to make decisions.

Employees need to be able to visualize what library services should be in the future. They can have this vision if they are participants in shaping the library's goals and if they have a part in developing the plans that are necessary to bring the library to these new levels. The resources are both human and inanimate, and they are dependent upon the library's financial support. These resources are the tools the staff needs in order to proceed on the path toward reaching the vision. Empowerment means a sharing of the power; the library manager, if a good leader, should be willing to do this. Leadership means getting things done through people, and this is what we must do if we are going to utilize our staffs as part of the internal training network.

Presentation and discussion of a vision is not a onetime event. To be effective, the vision must be communicated day in and day out. It should be considered to be a living force in the everyday operation of the library. A good vision is coherent and has the commitment of the staff. It is important to have unity of purpose and ownership of vision, so that staff members can relate the vision to their own values and aspirations, and they can participate through their accomplishments in helping the library achieve this vision. Thus, activity that supports this empowerment makes the employees believe that they are being enabled to act rather than being manipulated. This process in itself will become a long-range motivator for staff members.

Building the network or the team will develop the capacity of the members to create training with results that the participants truly deserve. The effective library director or manager is able to build a team of people who work collaboratively to achieve a common goal. This team is not found in organizational charts, but rather in their actual functions. Such efforts will produce a staff that will be productive consistently for a long time.

In addition to having a clear understanding of the mission and the vision of the library, staff members who are oriented to the library will also be able to understand the principles or guiding beliefs of the organization and then apply them in daily operations. Their everyday achievements are what the staff development coordinator should consider as the ongoing program of training planned for the employees.

In developing an overall plan for staff development, there should be a focused effort to evaluate what talents there are within the library system. Notice if there is someone who is able to maintain a sense of humor during difficult situations. Is there someone who writes especially good memos or outlines? Is there an individual who is particularly efficient and seems to get much more done than everyone else? These people should be considered when you are trying to develop training to meet specific needs that either the staff or the management has identified. Very often the solution to the training is right within our own organizations, and we overlook it because it is right there!

PRESENTATIONS

At first, some staff members from whom you would like presentations will be hesitant. They may never have spoken before a group, and they may not have the confidence in their own abilities to do the presentation. The very best way to convince them otherwise is to show them how to do the presentations by example. This works when the library director or the staff development person offers a workshop and simultaneously exhibits leadership. This will demonstrate training techniques that the other employees will then be able to use in the workshops they offer.

The following suggestions relate to what the trainer should take into consideration while developing a presentation. The first is presence. Body movements—including positioning at a podium, moving through an audience, using hands to emphasize points, and especially making eye contact during these presentations—are techniques that not only put the presenter at ease, but also serve to draw the audience into the performance. The voice is also an important tool for the presenter. The more variety there is in pitch, in volume, and in tempo, the more people the presenter will be able to attract. The length of the presentation must be considered in terms of covering the subject while holding the interest of the group. Content should consist of both the whys and the hows of the program, with most of the emphasis being on the how, but the rationale is also important. After all, this is the reason you are planning to hold the program in the first place.

In the planning of a presentation, the trainer should always set aside time for questions and answers. The trainer should not be intimidated by negative questions; there are always some. If you have done your homework, and are prepared for the workshop, you will be able to counter these negative comments with facts. Usually, the positive questions and comments will outweigh the negative ones. Those who are truly interested in the topic will bring forth great discussions.

TRAINING RESOURCES

In Chapter 10, the reader will find a variety of resources that will assist the person who is developing a training program. In addition, it is highly recommended that the trainer check the collection that is right within the library, in both print and nonprint resources. Local companies, colleges, and universities might have materials or staff that would also be of assistance in this process. Two exceptional books are Ross and Dewdney's *Communicating Professionally* and Daniels' *Organizational Communication*. Any prospective trainer would do well to review them before beginning the planning of presentations. Generally speaking, if one follows through with the models, and builds upon the information that is given, one will have the basic foundation for organizing the content of a training program.

IDENTIFYING TRAINERS

The library manager or staff development coordinator will be able to sense which staff members may be ready to begin this in-house training process. While it is important to provide many staffers with the opportunity to offer programs, you should be careful to begin your sessions with the most experienced people. It is very important to the long-range success of your staff training that you start out well. The staff members who participate in these early successes will be the best advertisement for the program. If they feel that they are valuable and that their time was well spent, they will carry that message to their colleagues and encourage them to participate as well. Unfortunately, the same is true if they are unhappy with the program. So, to be sure, put tremendous effort into offering a super program right off.

Effective trainers should exhibit most of the following attributes. The staff development coordinator should keep these in mind while searching for potential trainers.

AN EFFECTIVE TRAINER

1. is tactful, calm, and natural;
2. is open-minded and knowledgeable regarding the subject;
3. is authoritative to inspire confidence, trust, and respect;
4. has the ability to analyze accurately; is a quick thinker;
5. is objective, impersonal, and unbiased in thinking and able to stay on track;
6. is organized yet adaptable to a given situation;
7. has the ability to accept information and ideas from others;
8. is enthusiastic;
9. has a sense of humor;
10. is knowledgeable about human nature and patient with its various manifestations (grandstanding, etc.).

It would be a "superperson" who possessed all of these attributes, so please do not give up if there is no one on the staff who has all ten. The key to helping any one of them develop into a good trainer is to emphasize the five leadership characteristics they have and use them to the best advantage. It is also quite possible to pair two employees—to "team teach" a workshop. This gives you the option of drawing on their different personalities and abilities in order to find the right mix for the leadership of a particular training program.

As mentioned earlier, one of the roadblocks that the staff development organizer will inevitably come across is the hesitancy of the staff members to become trainers. Many of them will go so far as to tell you that they don't think that they are qualified for this type of activity. I think that it is incredibly helpful for staff members to be part of a workshop on positive self-image. This will not only present a way for them to develop their own confidence, but will also help us appreciate one another's skills. A reluctance that many individuals have about participating in homegrown types of programs stems from the belief that there is nothing that they can learn from their coworkers or that their coworkers can learn from them. This is so very, very wrong. The more presentations and workshops I lead, the more I realize how much I learn and benefit from the very people I am training. Regardless of the position that we hold in the library, we all can and do benefit from other people's perspectives and techniques if we keep an open mind. The next few pages contain a model program that has proven its effectiveness over the course of many years. Not only has it had positive results with employees, it has also been used successfully with other colleagues, both in this profession and in others, and with the members of community-based organizations. People are capable of far more than they think they are, and this program is designed to help them come to that realization.

I think that the most important thing about being an administrator is that we must remember that we are working with people. We must recognize that all people are different and they have different ways of dealing with the same situation. The most important rule that I have ever learned about working with people is that you handle people the way that you yourself would like to be handled. If you remember this, and use the model that follows, you will have begun the process of valuing employees, who will then begin to value themselves. It seems like such a small step, but in actuality it is a gigantic one toward successful staff development.

DEVELOPING POSITIVE SELF-IMAGE

Figure 4.1   Model Program

Developing a Positive Self-Image
I.   Introduction: We use only one-tenth of our potential.
   1.   This is a fact that has been proven by research.
   2.   While we think we are limited because of environment or social or economic backgrounds, the only real limit on us is ourselves.
   3.   Positive change cannot be given to you by any outside force—it must come from within yourself.
II. Defining Self-Image
   1.   Self-image is a mental picture that we have of ourselves. We have developed this image through our lives, with contributions (both positive and negative) from a variety of sources. These include but are not limited to our family life (our parents, siblings, spouses, and children), our workplace (our supervisors as well as those who are supervised by us), and other environmental influences (government, school systems, neighborhoods).
   2.   The image that you have of yourself must be one that you are comfortable with if you are going to be successful. The first step is to recognize how you feel about yourself. What are your strengths and weaknesses? What are your favorite things about yourself? Are there some things that you do not like and want to improve?
III. How to Make Those Improvements (Goal Setting)
   1.   You should force yourself to visualize what you want as your image, then develop actions to achieve it. This is important because the process forces you to set priorities and establishes a direction for your actions. Your self-image will automatically begin to improve as you begin to achieve even small steps toward your goal. Most important, this process will make you accept responsibility for your own life.
   2.   Goals should be written down because then they become more real to you. They should be *yours*, not someone else's, and should be stated in positive language. When you develop these goals for yourself, make them realistic and obtainable. While it seems good to "shoot for the stars," it is discouraging when you are not able to reach them. Better is to have some specific, real, reachable goals, which will in turn motivate you to set some new ones that are more ambitious.
   3.   Plan for your achievements. You should make a list of all of the obstacles that could possibly prohibit you from being successful, and look for alternative ways to reach your goal. Think of this as the same as taking a difficult route to work if you hear on the news that there is a traffic jam on the highway you normally take. Set a deadline for yourself. Without a schedule to follow, most of us will follow human nature and procrastinate. Create a desire in yourself to achieve. Give yourself rewards as you complete tasks. Evaluate how you are doing and make the changes necessary to keep you on the right path.
IV. Taking Charge
   1.   Action is the only way to make changes. The first step is always the hardest. Begin. If you find that you are not on the right path you can always change it.
   2.   A key to avoiding stress is not to worry about the small things. We have to learn to look beyond our own little niche and put these things in perspective.

Figure 4.1 Continued

V. Give Yourself Permission to Like Yourself
1. Appreciate yourself. You are an important person. You must do this before you can deal effectively with other people.
2. Do not be too hard on yourself or try to be perfect.
3. Do things that you enjoy, and emulate people you admire. Observing role models is a healthy way to learn new habits, as long as you are sure that that is the behavior you want to exhibit as your own.
4. Remember, however, no one's perfect. There is always room for improvement.

Figure 4.2 Sample Handout for Model Program

Your Attitude Toward Life: Your State of Mind When You Approach a Situation

Expectations:	What you think will happen
Perceptions:	What you think is happening
Self-image:	What you think about yourself
Self-confidence:	How you feel about your abilities
Acceptance:	Of yourself, of others, and of mistakes

Take a Positive Attitude Toward Yourself

Accept yourself, with your strengths and weaknesses. Do your best, using all your skills. Feel confident, show enthusiasm. Welcome change, growth, and new ideas. Have a sense of humor and keep things in perspective.

Take a Positive Attitude Toward Others

Be sincerely interested in others, their needs and their concerns.
Be a good listener. Give people your attention.
Respect others' points of view, even when you are not in agreement.
Work with others to achieve common goals.

Figure 4.3 Sample Handout: Developing an Achievement Mentality

The secret of success is believing you are capable of success.
The secret of success is having a clear focus—knowing exactly what you want and what you are willing to pay.
The secret of success is commitment to excellence. You will perform according to the way you value yourself.
The secret of success is responsibility for our own actions.
The secret of success is contributing to the world more than you take from it.
The secret of success is effort. There is no substitute for hard work.
The secret of success is to lead a balanced life, keeping things in priority and in perspective.

5 MENTORING AS A MEANS OF STAFF DEVELOPMENT

Mentoring can be achieved by pairing experienced employees with new or less experienced ones and is an often-overlooked method of providing staff development opportunities within our libraries. The first part of the process is to make sure that the overall work environment is one that provides an important venue for staff development. The environment must be supportive, open, and nonthreatening. Employees need to be reassured that making mistakes is a natural part of the learning process, and that their confidence in their abilities will improve with their experience. Practice and repetition reinforce the learning process, and observing the skills of experienced employees serves to help the new employees. Pairing provides checkpoints as well for the technique of the experienced employees, and showcases for their success. Mentors can oversee the work of the new employees and showcase their own skills at the same time.

The very best type of mentoring occurs when the relationship between new and experienced employees develops naturally. The chemistry between them makes them "click," and supportive relationships develop as a result. Modern trends in many organizations, however, include the institution of formal mentoring programs because they are so effective that the organizations cannot afford to wait for these relationships to happen by chance. One reason this type of program is so effective is the importance of role-modeling: exhibiting desirable behavior is one of the very best ways to encourage similar behavior in other employees. Another reason for the success of mentors is that the process provides employees with a humanizing dimension that makes a difference in the long-term development of organizational teamwork. Employees learn who they can approach for assistance in difficult situations or when they need answers to questions. Introductions and making contacts are other aspects of the mentoring situation. Introducing newcomers to others in the library organization or in the community is a mentor responsibility that makes the organization seem more human. Mentors can also help the newcomers become a part of the culture of the organization by explaining traditions and warning against difficult situations and politics. Because of the close working relationships that develop between mentors and "mentees," mentors are often in the best position to evaluate the work of new employees and report their progress to supervisors and administrators.

Mentor relations are really about professional success and personal growth. Mentors provide a safe haven for new employees, because they provide a way for these individuals to test situations, to ask questions, and to make mistakes without embarrassment, as long as there is still learning going on. Mentors can help formulate and guide work and career dreams. Mentoring becomes a responsibility for us in the profession when we begin to see work as more than a job—when we realize that we will be doing this for our entire lives. A way to reinforce and extend our career goals is to pass them on to others.

There are benefits in the mentoring process for the mentor as well as for the protégé. The fact is that the relationships are mutually beneficial if they are based on respect. The mentors begin to build power bases as individuals look up to them and as their good reputations spread. Mentors receive confirmation that their knowledge and experience are valuable. Mentoring gives us the opportunity to sit back and reflect on what we have learned and accomplished and to pass it on to another. This fits in with the classic definition of mentoring, which is the mutually beneficial relationship between two people which is based on the needs of both. It is a relationship that constantly changes and evolves. Ideally, the mentor wants her protégé to learn from her and then surpass her capabilities. Mentorships present opportunities for people to shape themselves and to look within themselves for answers.

There are different degrees and levels of mentoring relationships. The first level is between peers or colleagues. These relationships can provide a strong network of support and information among staff members, who can serve as sounding boards for one another. They can share experiences and inside information. They can compensate for one another's weakness as well as learn from one another. Peers can be very supportive mentoring partners, each filling the mentor and protégé roles at various times and in various situations.

The next level of a mentoring relationship grows from a trainer relationship. Providing day-to-day, hands-on involvement helps employees improve their performance and prepare themselves for further advancement. In these relationships, there has to be honesty and the ability to provide constructive criticism on behavior and performance. This type of relationship is goal oriented, focusing on developing skills and new strategies. The next step is when the trainer takes on further responsibility toward a particular employee and becomes his or her sponsor. In this relationship, the sponsor promotes the employee publicly, recognizing and drawing attention to skills and potential. The sponsor may make it possible for the employee to be put on special committees or task forces, receive promotions, or gain other recognition within the library or community.

In addition to being a role model who leads the way for employees, mentors are very important during the moments in an employee's career when decisions must be made. The mentor can help point out why a person would be good in a particular specialty, whether a try should be made for a promotion (IS he or she ready for it?), or even whether a career change should be considered. The mentor usually is in a position of power in the organization, and is able to provide behind-the-scenes information ("Don't accept that position in X library. Sally Jones is not returning in May, and you are being considered for that position"). Mentors are able to introduce employees to members of the power structure and can both protect them and lobby for special assignments for them. The mentor demonstrates the values and the standards of the profession while promoting and enhancing a sense of competence and confidence in the employee. Very often, too, it is the mentor who will cause the employee to stretch abilities, encouraging goals that the employee might have thought were beyond reach.

Mentors have the opportunity to receive a higher level of benefit from their peers because of having chosen to promote someone with potential. They gain respect because they have been developing talent, and the thriving of the new employee is a reflection of the mentor's good judgment. In many ways, being a mentor is a morale booster for experienced employees who may be suffering from burnout. The mentoring experience offers the opportunity to stay in touch with new developments in the field by talking and working with people who have only recently completed their formal learning. It offers the chance to reappraise past performance and to appreciate how one's own career has developed and even perhaps the chance to groom one's successor. When a person shares strength and wisdom, he or she becomes stronger, wiser, and more confident.

Finally, one should not overlook the benefits that the organization derives from encouraging and arranging mentoring opportunities. When mentoring succeeds, people have a sense of belonging and their teamwork and their productivity increase. They are less likely to leave because they feel a commitment to the organization as well as a loyalty to the person who has guided them. Communications are improved, and the mixing of styles strengthens the organization as newcomers are encouraged to apply different approaches and perspectives. It is also natural for smooth succession to evolve from mentoring.

In summary, four main steps of mentoring are 1. the initiation, when the mentor meets the new employee; 2. the cultivation, during which the employee learns from the mentor; 3. the separation, when the employee is able to move away from the mentor and branch out on his or her own; and 4. the redefinition, when the employee and the mentor can redesign their relationship, support one another, continue their friendship, and help someone else.

The wisdom one gains through experience must be passed on to others. It is not something that can be paid back; our debt is paid when we bring others along. The most important part of being a leader, in the final analysis, may be that you have prepared someone else to take your place.

Figure 5.1 is a form that can be distributed to staff members interested in becoming mentors. It is designed to help them take a hard look at themselves and decide if they would like to participate in such a program. Figure 5.3 is a checklist for the supervisor. It should be used as a guide to evaluate staff members to determine if they would be good matches for the task of mentoring particular individuals. This tool is especially useful during the hiring process. It makes you consider what personality traits one would need to fit in and complement those who are already a part of your organization.

Note: Sometimes the question is asked, "Is there a difference between a role model and a mentor?" The answer is yes. A role model may be emulated from a distance and does not necessarily take a mentoring responsibility.

Figure 5.1   Mentor Survey

Use this survey to evaluate yourself or appropriate staff members as possible mentors.

Check all that apply.

1. Which of the following best describes you?
    ____   experienced employee
    ____   high level of responsibility
    ____   on a fast track
    ____   independent
    ____   bored with job, looking for a challenge
    ____   potential role model
    ____   confident in career

2. Do you enjoy helping less experienced people by
    ____   teaching a specific skill?
    ____   helping them clarify goals?
    ____   introducing them to your organization?
    ____   providing specific information?
    ____   demonstrating their work?

3. Do you get a feeling of satisfaction in developing others by
    ____   recognizing potential in employees?
    ____   providing support and encouragement?
    ____   teaching a specific set of skills?
    ____   encouraging them to try something new?
    ____   giving recognition to improve confidence and self-esteem?
    ____   discussing and promoting their values?

4. Do you feel rewarded when helping others
    ____   develop a team?
    ____   provide leadership for the team?
    ____   improve skills?
    ____   improve performance?

5. Do you enjoy
    ____   counseling others?
    ____   giving advice?
    ____   providing encouragement?
    ____   providing recognition or praise?
    ____   recognizing the performance that is up to standard and providing strategies for improvement?
    ____   helping people to compensate for their limitations or those of the organization?

Figure 5.1 Continued

6. Are you able to
   ___ push people when they need it?
   ___ evaluate performance that does not meet expectations and recommend changes?
   ___ provide development opportunities?
   ___ assign people to difficult tasks and help them succeed?
   ___ match skills and abilities to organization's goals?

7. Are you able to help people with organizational structure by
   ___ clarifying goals and objectives?
   ___ showing them how to contribute to organizational success?
   ___ promoting service standards?
   ___ explaining opportunities for growth or promotion?

8. You want to help or teach others because
   ___ you want others to learn the profession.
   ___ you want to delegate responsibilities.
   ___ you want to increase your self-esteem as well as theirs.
   ___ you want to share your expertise.
   ___ you want to use the power of your position and reputation to help others.

If you checked at least one-half of these, chances are you would be a good mentor to or role model for new employees.

Figure 5.2   Hints for Being a Good Mentor

1. Know when to give instructions and when to give orders. Orders are appropriate when the employee knows how to complete a project that will meet your expectations and you need to have a job done. Instructions are appropriate when you need to explain how to do something to someone who has not done the job before or if it is a new method of doing things.
2. Tailor instruction to meet individual needs. Staff members have different levels of understanding; you must keep these in mind. Ask them to let you know if you are being too repetitive. Use a step-by-step process to explain.
3. Speak the same language. Avoid jargon unless you are sure the person knows this secret language of our profession.
4. Be specific. Explain *what* you want, *when* it is due, *what* you expect completed, what latitude the employee has in decision-making.
5. Demonstrate. Show the way so the employee can visualize what you want.
6. Explain why. If you explain why you are doing something, you help the employee understand how the project will affect the organization as a whole. This puts value on the task.
7. Stand and listen. Employees are valuable contributors to our organization—pay attention to what is said and always read between the lines.
8. Provide feedback. Let employees know you are satisfied with their work. If something is not right, give an explanation of why it is not and determine what caused the problem so it can be corrected.

Figure 5.3   Characteristics of Good Mentors

Accessible	Accurate
Competent	Nurturing
Successful	Supportive
Respectful	Protective
Good teachers and motivators	Aggressive
Inspire confidence	Assertive
Empathetic	Risk taking
Honest	Generous (with credit, praise)

What the Protégé Looks for in the Mentor

Compatibility	Availability
Expertise	Honesty
Admiration	Teacher
Behavior	Sounding board
Professional values	Cheerleader
Emotional involvement	Friend
Door openings	Inspiration

What the Mentor Looks for in the Protégé

Promise	Desire to learn; ambition
Potential	Commitment
Loyalty	Accepts challenge

6 DAY-TO-DAY BASICS FOR MANAGERS

All organizations, whether they are nonprofit like libraries or profit-making businesses, have a tremendous need for an innovative, creative work force. As an administrator, you need to be able to influence others and to shape events and activities within your workplace in order to achieve the organization's goals. People are basically eager to know what job you want them to do and what standards you have for good performance. People want to succeed, and they become even more motivated by success because they feel competent. People who feel good about themselves are more willing to act and try new ideas more readily.

Effective training means that there will be some lasting and detectable change in the behavior of the individuals. Its value is that it helps us make our staffs more productive using fewer resources.

Whether we intend to or not, all of our organizations pay for training. Not having a structured program in place means that your organization pays for training day by day on the job in a way that makes it more costly and inefficient. It is much better and more economical to have an efficient training program in place. Investing quality time and money into training will have great payoffs for you over the years. You reduce the time that it takes people to get up to speed, and you reduce the likelihood of mistakes.

We need to remember that a job is simply a set of defined tasks and that it has a relationship with other jobs within the organization. The critical part of any training is making our employees understand their jobs in the context of the total operation. If we keep this in mind, we will help our employees understand and believe in their value within the organization. This will lead them and the organization to success.

Staff development is a tool with which to organize and control work so that it achieves intended results. The administrator's commitment to staff development is required to unleash the energy of the work force and to hold it accountable.

STAFF EMPLOYMENT STANDARDS

Customizing the description of our employee's work both will help us achieve the required results and will also serve to challenge the abilities of the particular person who is holding the job. Combining the customized description with training gives individuals the independence and freedom to be innovative and to develop and channel their energies and skills to the advantage of the library system. Improvisation and enhancement require mastery of the basics of a job just as in music.

In describing positions we must be able to provide established boundaries while at the same time encourage employees to pursue their strengths. These descriptions are best when fluid and adaptable. The following are some areas that should be included in the attempt to describe tasks:

1. Work functions—what will the person do?
2. Accountable results—what will be produced as a result of work over a given period?
3. Strengths—what are the major abilities that an individual should possess that can be channeled toward achieving intended results?
4. Motivators—what energies will drive the individual toward the required results?
5. Limitations—what are unacceptable actions and lines that cannot be crossed?
6. Resources—what know-how is available, what tools, information sources, etc., can an individual use to achieve results?
7. Delegated decisions—What level of authority has been delegated to the employee to make decisions without checking with someone else?
8. Consultative decisions—what type of decision must be checked with a supervisor before it can be executed?
9. Prescribed activities—what tasks *must* the individual perform according to the organization's philosophy?
10. Responsibility potential—what are the implications for new responsibilities to be assigned (i.e., what is the promotion potential?)?

Because results and accountability have taken on paramount importance and seem likely to take on even more in the workplace of the next century, we can see the increased necessity for continuing staff development and training within our organizations. The focus has shifted to performance and production, and the changing nature of our practice requires that results become every person's responsibility. Periodic assessment of these results sets up the performance review process within our system. Results are what we ultimately will reward and compensate. The following pages are intended to provide some actual, hands-on advice that can be used by the library administrator and passed on to other supervisors and trainers. As has been earlier stated, it is absolutely essential that these are viewed as guidelines and be adjusted and adapted to fit the needs of the particular library in which you manage.

HINTS FOR DEVELOPING SUCCESSFUL TRAINING

We get better at tasks the more we practice them. Staff development training is like anything else. The more often that we offer programs, the better able we are to anticipate the needs of our staffs, select trainers to carry out the workshops, and project the impacts and outcomes of the situations. The following pages include many suggestions to assist you in becoming more comfortable with beginning a staff development program within your library. Once you begin, you will no doubt find shortcuts and methods that work well for you and will make the process of staff development become second nature to you.

- Take care with the quality of training that the library offers. It must project the administration's concerns and professionalism. The quality of training sends a strong message to staff about the quality of the organization.
- Every trainer must have a clear understanding of what the expected outcome of the training is in order to do a good job.
- Encourage staff members to become trainers. One of the very best ways of mastering a subject is to teach it to someone else.
- Trainers must always remember to be themselves; being anything else is a mistake.
- Trainers must learn to become task competent, that is they must develop the skills, knowledge, and relevant experience for specific tasks so they can share them with others.
- Trainers must be interpersonally competent. They must be socially skillful and able to sense feelings of individuals and of the group as a whole and to be personally persuasive.
- Good trainers practice, either in front of a mirror or with

a small circle of family or friends. Practicing is a part of preparation.

- Practice what you teach. Good trainers are good role models and use the skills they want others to imitate.
- Make supportive handouts and resources available.
- Use audiovisual media appropriately to enhance presentations. Be certain that they work and that you are fully in control of them. Never show any material to a group which you have not heard or viewed yourself.

TRAINING HINTS: USING AUDIOVISUAL AIDS

In today's world we are continually bombarded with multimedia messages, and many people have become used to them, finding presentations without the use of some audiovisual aids hard to follow and even boring. There are many types of commercial media available to you; however, it is also not difficult to add a video clip of your library or an overhead or some other prop to break up the presentation. I have included some specific hints to assist you and the trainers in making audiovisuals become a routine part of presentations.

- Use large charts, slides, overlays, or videos projected onto a large screen.
- Use color to distinguish categories or to highlight.
- Pictures and drawings require interpretation and are not easily grasped. Be selective.
- Key features should occupy at least a half of the screen, chart, or display. Do not include secondary details. Keep it simple.
- Maintain eye contact with your audience even when using visuals, or you will lose them.
- Parallel your flow of words with the flow of visuals. Disjointed concepts can be confusing.
- Flip charts support spoken presentations and let the audience participate as they silently read the copy you have prepared.
- Overhead projectors can show large images to a large audience. You can also add information to the prepared overhead slides by marking them with special markers, or

adding transparencies to the basic slides, as you do the presentation.

- 35mm slides need to be used in a darkened room, but they are very useful in presenting materials that are impossible to describe verbally. If you are going to use them, however, you must know your presentation without referring to notes because it will be too dark to read.
- Sound (music, sound effects, and professional voices) can be added to the presentation for additional impact.
- Prerecorded messages eliminate stammers, stutters, and wasted time. They maintain a level of enthusiasm and zest throughout the performance because they have been edited, unlike live presentations. They are also especially useful when you want to extract a message or quote from a famous person.
- Videotape has the advantage of conveying your message exactly the same way each time it is shown. It is the most versatile of all the media because it combines many elements of good communication (movement, color, language, sound, and often music).

An audiovisual aid is a training tool. It should not take the place of a carefully planned presentation by a live presenter. The limitation common to all of the canned formats is that the staff is not able to interact with the presenter. Distance learning is addressing this shortfall and has its uses, but I am not convinced it will ever replace direct human contact.

Starting a new program can be overwhelming. It is often helpful to talk with colleagues about their experiences: what worked, what did not work, and why. Consider the following pages by going through the development programs and implementing and evaluating them. These are basic and certainly not all-inclusive lists. They are not intended to be step-by-step guides, but rather a reminder of some of the types of management techniques that we can apply to staff development programming. Giving feedback, building teams, and solving problems are all parts of the day-to-day responsibilities of an administrator. The manager's self-audit will help you assess your abilities and point out areas in which you may need to strengthen skills. These hints should help you avoid some of the pitfalls that can destroy your enthusiasm for a staff development program within your library.

THINGS TO REMEMBER WHILE TRAINING AND ORGANIZING TRAINING

Keeping these things in mind while you are training will keep you inspired and help you motivate others. When all is said and done, what do you want the training to be remembered for? Individuals must accept the responsibility for their own development. You, as the trainer, can assist them to gain skills and knowledge, but the focus must come from within. Teachers or trainers often learn far more than their students. Keep an open mind while you are training. Helping others develop is one of the ways that we can continue to develop ourselves.

STEPS TO LEAD YOUR LIBRARY TO SUCCESS

1. Be enthusiastic; it is infectious.
2. Work hard, but take the time to enjoy what you do.
3. Go above and beyond what is expected. Leading means that you move out in front of the others so that they will strive to catch up with you.
4. Share the credit for success with others who are a part of your organization in any way (board members and friends as well as staff).
5. Shoulder failures alone. Ultimately, the measure of your strength will be how you reorganize after a crisis. Hold yourself accountable.
6. Make sure you can take pride in your performance.
7. Don't demand from your employees anything that you would not demand from yourself.

BUILDING A TEAM THAT WORKS

CHECKLIST FOR MANAGERS

1. Choose the right people for the jobs.
   a. Interview to find out what they are really like.
   b. Choose action people.
2. Make new members team members at the outset.
   a. Brief them on informal rules and customs.
   b. Let them know they are important and welcome to the team.

3. Train to achieve immediate results.
   a. Share the library's objectives.
   b. Find out what newcomers already know.
   c. Provide information on how they are doing; feedback and encouragement are vital.
4. Delegate. Share responsibility and authority to get a job done.
5. Create opportunities for your staff members to be partners in change to increase the action orientation of their outlook.
6. Understand the prevailing mood of the staff.
7. Build consensus by making sure everyone understands what is going on.
8. Manage by support and encouragement.
9. Lead by inspiring and encouraging others to work for solutions and set the standard for excellence by example.

HELPING STAFF MAINTAIN PERSPECTIVE

1. Make a list of staff accomplishments. Seeing the positive will help staff members see that all is not lost just because they are facing a little problem.
2. Emphasize that they need to have enough information to see the whole picture.
3. Point out that blaming others and buck-passing costs a lot of energy, time, and motivation, and it really interferes with progressive action.
4. Discourage procrastination by setting reasonable deadlines and standards.
5. Teach employees to look at tasks in series of steps. When tasks are broken down, they are not nearly so overwhelming. Each step accomplished should make those remaining easier.
6. Encourage employees to list pluses and minuses of situations; this will help them see situations as they really are.
7. Remember that when you stop learning on the job you begin to shrink. If you are overworked, put an extra stimulus on different tasks to keep you growing.
8. Create strategies that will help staff deal with pressures rationally.

GIVING FEEDBACK THAT WILL BE ACCEPTED

Many people are modest or even suspicious about accepting compliments and praise; however, sharing the good things is as important as solving any problem. Here are some hints for making your praise more acceptable:

1. Be as specific as you can and explain the benefit of actions for your library.
2. Be as quick as possible so that you do not embarrass the staff member.
3. Don't allow the person to say, "It was nothing." Interrupt (politely, of course) with a smile and say something like, "Don't try to talk me out of praising you."
4. Be sincere. Pay attention to the activities and specify exactly what was done rather than using a generic "Great job!"
5. Make praise personal and individualized.
6. Know when to praise in public and when it is more appropriate to praise privately.

KEYS TO SUCCESSFUL PROBLEM-SOLVING

1. Stay objective.
2. Determine what actually happened.
3. Ask for suggestions from employees and advice from colleagues.
4. Evaluate suggestions and advice and put only the best to use.
5. Follow up on results to see if the solution has solved the problem.
6. Make sure that you reward good performance, but not poor or nonperformance, and make sure that all employees have received the message that their performance matters.
7. Remember that if you are making mistakes, you are taking risks and trying to make intelligent choices; you won't get anywhere unless you do.
8. Accept certain elements that defy immediate solution so you can begin to change things for the better.

A MANAGER'S SELF-AUDIT: WHAT IT TAKES TO BECOME A COMPETENT LEADER

Leaders are action oriented:
They plan, set priorities, and implement.
They keep things moving.
They are concerned with impact and results rather than with getting bogged down by process. They get the job done.
They are analytical and systematic.
They make tough decisions.
Leader skills and characteristics:
They are self-confident.
They conceptualize and set goals.
They are strong communicators.
They are able to manage a group process.

They are objective and listen to all sides of an issue.
They are self-controlled and tolerant.
They possess stamina and good humor.
Leaders are supervisors:
They accept responsibility and are accountable.
They genuinely want to help others develop.
Leaders are successful when they use their time efficiently to mobilize others to perform. The best leaders of all are the ones who are able to help people who follow them to outgrow them and become leaders themselves.

WAYS FOR MANAGERS TO ACHIEVE RESULTS

1. Focus on your goals.
2. Keep control without interfering by delegating.
3. Choose the right people.
4. Challenge people to take on new experiences.
5. Don't dump jobs on employees.
6. Share responsibility and power.
7. Delegate gradually.
8. Gain commitment by involving people in the process.
9. Learn from mistakes.
10. Keep employees involved.
11. Do things right and do the right thing.
12. Set an example that will encourage people to trust and support you.

HOW TO ACCOMPLISH SPECIFIC JOB TRAINING

1. Clear, dynamic position descriptions are the first step to job training and staff development.
2. A written statement of performance expectation should be given to all employees.
3. Concentrate on teaching simple tasks first.
4. Break tasks down into components to make them more easily understood and achievable.
5. Keep teaching cycles short and reinforce the teaching by practice.
6. Develop skills through hands-on practice and repetition.
7. Develop strengths and capacities into required skills.
8. Motivate trainees with motivated trainers.

TIPS FOR MANAGERS ON TEAMBUILDING

1. Your mission statement must be concise, clear, and communicated.
2. Your corporate thinking expresses what you stand for. This

is a statement of values expressed positively, and you should write it as you intend to live it.

3. Your values govern your day-to-day operational philosophy.
4. Your goals determine how you will use all the resources.
5. The staff's performance reflects the organization's philosophy.
6. Rituals and traditions create goodwill—ties that bind employees to the organization and create a sense of unity.

LEADERSHIP TRAITS

Leadership traits that motivate others to follow your direction are vision, the ability to innovate, focus, decision-making skill, rationality, the ability to handle pressure, trustworthiness, a sense of humor, encouraging involvement, demonstrated convictions of principles, and persistence.

This chapter is intended to provide you with some food for thought. Further assistance can certainly be obtained through graduate courses in management and through individualized learning and reading. There is a wealth of material on the topic: some specific to libraries; others that, although intended for business or other types of companies, are wonderful, proven strategies for managers. Good managers must keep themselves aware of the changes within the management field. In our case, we can use the resources we provide our patrons to help us do this. Coupled with the materials that are found in the other chapters of this manual, the library director should be able to proceed with a staff development program right at home—in the library.

7 MODEL STAFF DEVELOPMENT PROGRAMS

The aim of this manual is to provide assistance to library managers. It should help them to develop strategies to provide the necessary day-to-day training situations that arise in their organizations. The models that follow are meant to be a resource in this. Training is crucial if our library's employees are going to achieve a uniform standard of performance. We want our service to be the same every hour we are open, not just when a particular employee is "on desk." No two librarians are the same, just as no two people are the same, so I would strongly recommend that these materials be used as they were intended—as models. In order for your program to reach maximum effectiveness, you will want to adapt and change portions of the models to make them more suitable for your needs. In addition, be sure to coordinate your program so that it will focus on those areas which are most critical for you.

CHOOSING A TRAINING TOPIC

The best topic to choose for training involves areas of service that need improvement in the institution's approach to customers or potential customers. These needs should have been identified during the assessment process. Below is a list of possible topics that are appropriate for staff development programs. It is by no means all inclusive, but is presented to get your library thinking about possible course selections. After the selection of the topic, the next step is to use the appropriate resources to complete the training outline provided in Figure 7.1. This tool provides a preparation checklist that will prompt the trainer to complete all the details as he or she develops the plan.

The library's overall commitment to a continuing staff development program and the needs-assessment process will determine how many programs the library should offer, how often to offer them, and their length. These are the types of details that can be determined only within each library.

TRAINING TOPICS FOR STAFF DEVELOPMENT

Collecting Oral Histories
Communicating Effectively
Creating Good Impressions
Crisis Training
Customer Service
Dealing with Angry Patrons
Dealing with Conflicting Personalities
Developing Intergenerational Family Programming
Effective Building Maintenance
Getting Control of Your Time
Getting There: Goalsetting
Getting Things Done
Humor in the Workplace
Maintaining Equipment
Managing Capable People
Managing Collections
Multicultural Service
New Technologies
Organizing Family History Days
Orientation for New Employees
People Problems in Public Service
Personal Development
Relationships with Friends
Relationships with Staff Colleagues
Relationships with Trustees
Safety, Security, and Sensibility
Self-Esteem Development
Serving on Committees
Stress Management
Teamwork
Using Informed Judgment
Working Smart
Working with Volunteers

The following pages include sample training program models that can be used as is or adapted to any library. The first, "Communicating Effectively," is designed to improve both the internal communication of the library and the oral and written communication that the library uses with the rest of the world. Figure 7.2 is a way to evaluate the status of communication within the library. It should be completed by the director and then by as many staff members as possible. One of the interesting findings may be that the director and the staff members perceive the communication differently. In this case a red flag should go up indicating that there is a communication gap. The results of this audit will help the trainer develop the curriculum that he or she will use for the training. Training of this type is best done when the trainer has at least two hours to spend with the staff. It can be even more effective if the training can be carried out over two two-hour sessions. The handouts that are provided as examples can be given to the participants at the conclusion of the first session, with the intent that they be completed and brought with them to start off the second session. The methods of training that will be used for this or any topics will vary by trainer. In communication training, however, I like to use taped (audio and video) examples to illustrate both good and poor communication situations. Role-playing would be especially useful to use along with section III of this outline. All training sessions need to have a period of summary or conclusion, which will tie up loose ends, allow participants to ask questions, and set direction for implementation.

Figure 7.1   Sample Training Outline

Training Topic (Title of Subject):

Training Target (Who are you training? how many?):

Training Time (Length of program):

Training Objective (What is the intended result?):

I. (Broad content area)

   A. (Heading)

      1. (Subheading)   Training techniques _____

         a. (Topic)   Training aids needed _____

         b. (Topic)

   B. (Heading)

      1. (Subheading)   Training techniques _____

         a. (Topic)   Training aids needed _____

II. (Broad content area)

   A. (Heading)

      1. (Subheading)   Training techniques _____

         a. (Topic)   Training aids needed _____

COMMUNICATING EFFECTIVELY

TRAINING OUTLINE

I. Why is effective communication so necessary?
  A. People need to understand one another.
    1. They need to transfer information and get a point across.
    2. They need to create working relationships; they work with a better attitude.
  B. An atmosphere of caring and concern is created by communication.
    1. It helps us realize that because others care, we are willing to share.
    2. Openness eliminates misunderstanding.

II. What is communication all about?
  A. People understanding one another.
    1. Communication is designed to produce response.
    2. Feedback is response, and it indicates how well a message was received.
  B. Communication is about relationships; it is a two-way process.
    1. There is a sender and a receiver. Listening is after all one-half of the process.
    2. Every person communicates according to his or her ability to understand.
  C. Communication is a people process.
    1. Thought and feeling will indicate if you are on common ground.
    2. Maturity will lead you to withhold judgment until you have enough facts and will cause you to listen respectfully even when you are not in agreement.

III. What are the barriers that affect the communication process?
  A. Sender barriers
    1. Attitude about the message or the receivers.
    2. Poor communication skills—including unclear vocabulary and an inappropriate time, place, or method of delivering the message.
    3. Prejudices.
    4. Style.
  B. Receiver barriers
    1. Attitude about the message or the sender, including distrust and fear.
    2. Message is too complicated.

      3. The person is preoccupied and not really listening or understanding.

  C. Communication breakdown happens if

      1. The sender does not check for feedback regarding understanding of the message.

      2. The receiver indicates understanding has taken place when it really hasn't.

IV. Tips for being a good communicator

  A. Make the receiver feel as if he or she is the only person in the world.

      1. Be sensitive and aware.

      2. Take an interest in others.

      3. Smile.

  B. Know what you need to say

      1. Be specific and direct.

      2. Keep message clear in terms that will be understood.

      3. Be positive.

  C. The key to the receiver being interested is the need for information; interest in sender.

      1. Accept the fact that people do things for their own reasons.

      2. Adjust the message to meet the circumstances.

  D. Be yourself

      1. Be sincere.

      2. Don't pretend to know something you do not or to be something you are not.

V. Conclusion

  A. Communication is a two-way process.

  B. The value of the experience of communication is enhanced by applying the principles.

Figure 7.2   Communicating Effectively

Before holding the training, the manager should evaluate the way the organization is communicating internally and externally. This will help provide some relevant examples for the trainer. The audit may also result in disclosing the reason there is a perceived need for further improving communication.

Library Communication Audit

Always Often   Never

_____ _____ _____   1. Are regular newsletters provided for all employees?

_____ _____ _____   2. Are all staff members given advance notice of library-related functions?

_____ _____ _____   3. Are internal committees used for projects?

_____ _____ _____   4. Are the media informed of staff accomplishments?

_____ _____ _____   5. Is the library represented at community meetings?

_____ _____ _____   6. Are staff members involved in planning?

_____ _____ _____   7. Does the staff membership know the library board and vice versa?

_____ _____ _____   8. Do supervisors relate what is happening at meetings?

_____ _____ _____   9. Are regular staff meetings held?

_____ _____ _____   10. Is time made for informal discussions between staff and administration?

Training Objective: To improve the basic process of communication in order to help people help one another.

Training Methods to Be Used: Discussions, role-playing, brainstorming

Training Aids: Blackboard or flip chart, handouts

Figure 7.3   Handout for Communication Training

I. The Tools of Communication
    Being able to listen to another person
    Being able to write a letter of thanks
    Being able to write a note to just say hello
    Being able to write a letter of confirmation or a follow-up to what you have agreed to verbally
    Being able to write directions
    Being able to write instructions
    Being able to use the telephone wisely
    Being able to leave complete messages so that the receiver understands even if he or she has not talked with you in person

II. The World of Today Communicates by:
    Person-to-person meetings each day
    Telephones
    Internet and other electronic access, including fax machines.
    Television
    Radio
    Movies and video documentaries
    Program performances
    Newspapers
    Magazines and other print resources
    CDs, audiotapes

III. How Can I Become a Good Communicator?
    1. Be a person who cares for others and conveys it.
    2. Show that you have a positive attitude and you are excited about living.
    3. Write little notes and memos—they matter.
    4. Write letters for all reasons.
    5. Use the telephone efficiently.
    6. Train yourself to sit down more often and listen to what another person is telling you.
    7. Keep working at it. Some things will become routine, but continual communicating is important.

Figure 7.4   Communication Handout

Use the following evaluation to check your communication skills.

	Yes	No	I need improvement
1. I pay attention when introduced to others and therefore remember their names.	____	____	____
2. I smile when around other people, and they usually smile back.	____	____	____
3. I resist opportunities to beat my own drum, and I'm considered modest by my friends.	____	____	____
4. I look for opportunities to compliment others.	____	____	____
5. I am interested in others and what they have to say.	____	____	____
6. I notice little things like birthdays and remember them.	____	____	____
7. I avoid arguments at all costs.	____	____	____
8. If I must criticize, I begin with a positive statement or praise.	____	____	____
9. I restate points of agreement whenever there may be a conflict.	____	____	____
10. I give the other person opportunities to bow out gracefully or save face.	____	____	____
11. I don't put myself above others by saying things like, "I told you so."	____	____	____
12. I ask questions designed to produce the answers I need.	____	____	____
13. I ask questions and make requests instead of giving orders.	____	____	____
14. I organize my thoughts before I speak.	____	____	____
15. I always try to use terms that are familiar to my listener.	____	____	____
16. I try to be as specific as possible when I speak.	____	____	____
17. I realize that communication is most accurate when it is kept simple.	____	____	____
18. I am aware of the gestures and phrases I use.	____	____	____
19. I realize people do things for their reasons, not mine.	____	____	____
20. I always try to act naturally, admit my mistakes, and show my sincerity through my actions.	____	____	____

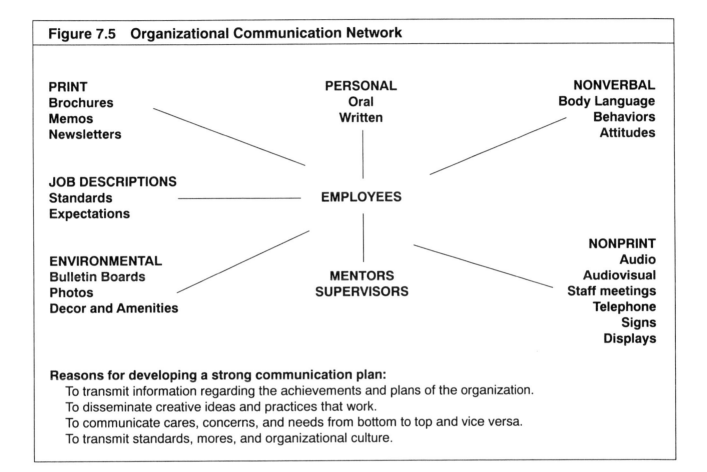

Figure 7.5   Organizational Communication Network

PRINT
Brochures
Memos
Newsletters

PERSONAL
Oral
Written

NONVERBAL
Body Language
Behaviors
Attitudes

JOB DESCRIPTIONS
Standards
Expectations

EMPLOYEES

ENVIRONMENTAL
Bulletin Boards
Photos
Decor and Amenities

MENTORS
SUPERVISORS

NONPRINT
Audio
Audiovisual
Staff meetings
Telephone
Signs
Displays

Reasons for developing a strong communication plan:
　To transmit information regarding the achievements and plans of the organization.
　To disseminate creative ideas and practices that work.
　To communicate cares, concerns, and needs from bottom to top and vice versa.
　To transmit standards, mores, and organizational culture.

ORIENTATION PROGRAMS

The following program is an example of one that is useful to offer to new employees. It can be done either in a group or on a one-to-one basis, depending on the institutional needs. Orientation programs serve both the employee and the organization. They provide a means for the introduction of newcomers to the staff and policies of their new employer; it provides a way to make the newcomers feel comfortable in their new environment; and it provides a way for the library to explain all of the institutional "housekeeping" that is always necessary. If the employer has an employee handbook or other written manual, this would be an appropriate time for distribution. There are some sample handouts that can be used for this if the library does not have a manual of its own. Depending upon the size of the organization, I would recommend a four- to eight-hour orientation program. Spending a little bit more time at the outset will save much more time later on. It would also be appropriate to have the employee rotate through the various departments of the system to become familiar with the entire operation. Time for this will vary, but a minimum of a few days is really necessary for the person to absorb the knowledge.

Training Objective:	To provide information to employees to assist them in the performance of their specific jobs.
Program Purpose:	To communicate the organizational philosophy, mission, and goals and to provide clear expectations to new employees.
Training Methods:	Individual or small group sessions, discussion, and questions and answers followed up by on-site training.
Training Aids:	Handouts, organizational videos, and slide shows.
Evaluation:	Adaptation of new employees to the organization; one-on-one sessions between employees and supervisors at end of probationary period.

Figure 7.6   Training Curriculum

I. Philosophy Statement
  A. History and Achievements of the Library
    1. Important achievements
    2. Current status
    3. Future directions, goals, and objectives
  B. Mission Statement
    1. Provides employees with a broad perspective on the organization
    2. Sets the stage for the employees' participation in helping library achieve it
    3. Includes things that make your library unique
  C. Sample Philosophy Inclusions
    1. Teamwork: Good library service results when it's everyone's job
    2. Treat employees like patrons—with respect and courtesy
    3. Quality: Do the job right
    4. Value: Make people feel they are getting their money's worth
II. Library Standards, Procedures, and Policies
  A. Standards
    1. Clearly written statements of expectations
    2. Performance standards as they relate to job descriptions
  B. Procedures and Policies
    1. Overview of the operations
    2. Operations manual
    3. Employee's role within the division or department
III. Employment Logistics
  A. Tour of the facility
    1. Floor-plan, evacuation plan overview, smoking areas, lounge facilities
    2. Staff introductions
  B. Employee Benefits
    1. Detail of the employee's contract
    2. Overview of general benefits and pay periods
  C. Chain of Command
IV. Library Opportunities
  A. Opportunities for Development
    1. Internal seminars, courses
    2. Participation in workshops, seminars, and conferences
    3. Encouragement of formal education and explanation of reimbursement policies
  B. Opportunities for Advancement
    1. Probationary period
    2. Promotion possibilities
V. On-Site Training
  A. Position Training
    1. Responsibilities defined
    2. Supervised jobs
  B. Library Training
    1. Cross-training with other departments
    2. Relationships between departments

Figure 7.6 Continued

VI. Evaluation
  A. Performance Evaluations
    1. Each employee is different and will respond to the training based on his or her own motivation, intelligence, personality, and willingness to work
    2. Training should send a message to the employee about the quality, caring and professionalism of the organization
  B. Conclusion
    1. The training should result in the employee's feeling more comfortable with the job
    2. Supervisors have the opportunity to make assessment of employee's abilities and skills and determine if employee is appropriately matched to the position
    3. Administration's most important decision is to select people and determine their performance capabilities. Failure to train them properly can have devastating consequences: poor performances, low productivity, need for increased supervision, heightened employee turnover, discipline and motivation problems in the workplace.

TEAMWORK

Every organization is more successful when the people within it are able to work together as a team. The teamwork training program can be used as a follow-up to the orientation training, or it can be used as a refresher course for employees who have been with the organization for a while. It is especially good to do with every department head or supervisor, and then have each one use newly learned skills to develop a team. It is training that can be implemented over a period of time, rather than in one two-hour training slot. A word of advice: Teamwork training is not something that can be done once and then forgotten. As with any sports team, there must be an ongoing coaching process. To be effective, the library director must recognize this need for continual coordination and direction.

TEAMWORK TRAINING CURRICULUM
  I. How to Build the Team
    A. Identify the organization's goals
      1. What is the job?
      2. What are you trying to do?
    B. All must have a clear understanding of their tasks and responsibilities
      1. What will help get the job done?
      2. What will hamper us from getting the job done?
  II. How to Identify the Strengths of the Employees
    A. Inventory each person's strengths

        1. Match strengths with activities
        2. Force each individual to look beyond the scope of his or her own efforts and consider how their strengths fit into the scope of things
    B. Learn from one another
        1. Breakdown status differentials
        2. Recognize that status is based on experience, but that every person has worthwhile contributions to make and needs the opportunity to reach potential

III. Adopt Participatory Management as Guide
    A. Everyone has the duty and responsibility to influence decision-making
        1. People need to understand the diversity of individual people's gifts
        2. People must trust and respect one another
    B. Participatory management provides the environment that allows momentum to develop
        1. An aggressive, professionally driven organization will result
        2. Team members will be able to make a meaningful difference in their organization
        3. Lead by examples so that your style is copied and passed on to other people
        4. You want constructive discontent

IV. The Team Needs to Help Develop the Vision
    A. Vision is about what the organization could and should be
        1. All who have a stake in the organization participate in creating the vision
        2. Leadership includes figuring out the right thing to do to approach the vision
    B. Strategies need to be rooted in understanding
        1. Fiscal considerations
        2. Personnel resources matter in order to produce change

V. Building a Strong Implementation Network
    A. Leadership involves risk-taking
        1. There are unknown consequences
        2. Risk-taking can be motivating and thus influence teambuilding
    B. Strategies for teamwork success
        1. Supportive relationships with key sources and resources
        2. Cooperative environment
        3. Motivation to make visions become reality

VI. Conclusion
    A. Leaders leave behind them assets and a legacy so that someone else can take over
    B. Leaders are obligated to create a team of followers whose lives and work are intertwined so that they can reach a goal

---

Figure 7.7   Handout: Getting the Most Out of Training

Before Attending

Research has shown that training is more effective if it is preceded and followed by discussions with one's supervisor. They should discuss what they hope to gain from the program and how it will change their job performance. Individuals should think about what problems they might be able to find solutions for by interacting with other participants.

Some Participation Tips

Much of the success of a program in terms of usefulness to the participants depends on their attitude. All participants should:
  1. Enter into discussions and talk with other participants.
  2. Be willing to learn from the experience.
  3. Meet with new people.
  4. Search for new ideas.
  5. Listen carefully to the subject content.
  6. Get involved as much as possible when there are activities.
  7. Use time well.
  8. Refer to the objectives of the program, and think, "How can I use this in my work?"

After Attending

The employee should talk with the supervisor about the training. Each should be asked if the program was up to expectations and how newfound knowledge will be used. All should be encouraged to ask the supervisor for support as they begin to apply their new skills. The supervisor should check back over the next few months to see if they have followed through with what they learned and to determine if further training is necessary.

Figure 7.8   Handout: Welcome!

Everyone has new job jitters. It is normal to wonder if you'll fit in, or if you will like the job, or if you will be able to perform it well. Accept the fact that it will be confusing at first and do not be too hard on yourself! Here are some things to do to help reduce the confusion of your new workplace.

1. Take some time to explore the library and observe the staff in action. Familiarity with the facility will help you reduce your fear of the unknown, and it will help you prepare for what you should expect.
2. Learn the basics as quickly as you can. Use introductions as a chance to gather useful information about your new coworkers. You'll be able to find out what people do, and you will begin to understand how your work will relate to them.
3. When in doubt, ask for advice or direction. Most people are especially kind to new employees because they remember what it was like for them.
4. Avoid developing a reputation as a critic. If you think of ways to improve current procedures, wait for the appropriate time to share them. People appreciate fresh points of view, but do not necessarily want to be told that the way they have been doing things is wrong.
5. Service to patrons is our first priority. You are joining a staff whose prime objective is to provide the very best possible library service. Keep the patron in mind, and you will do just fine.

Figure 7.9   Teamwork

Training Objective:	To develop effective teams in order to reach objectives.
Program Purpose:	An organization's success is determined by the attitudes, behavior, and performance of all our employees. Working together will provide a more efficient way of accomplishing our goals.
Training Methods:	Small group sessions with brainstorming; handouts; mentoring.
Training Aids:	Motivational posters and tapes.
Evaluation:	Performance of the library is measured against the job requirement fulfillments and the perceptions of performance standards.

Figure 7.10   Teamwork Planning Wheel

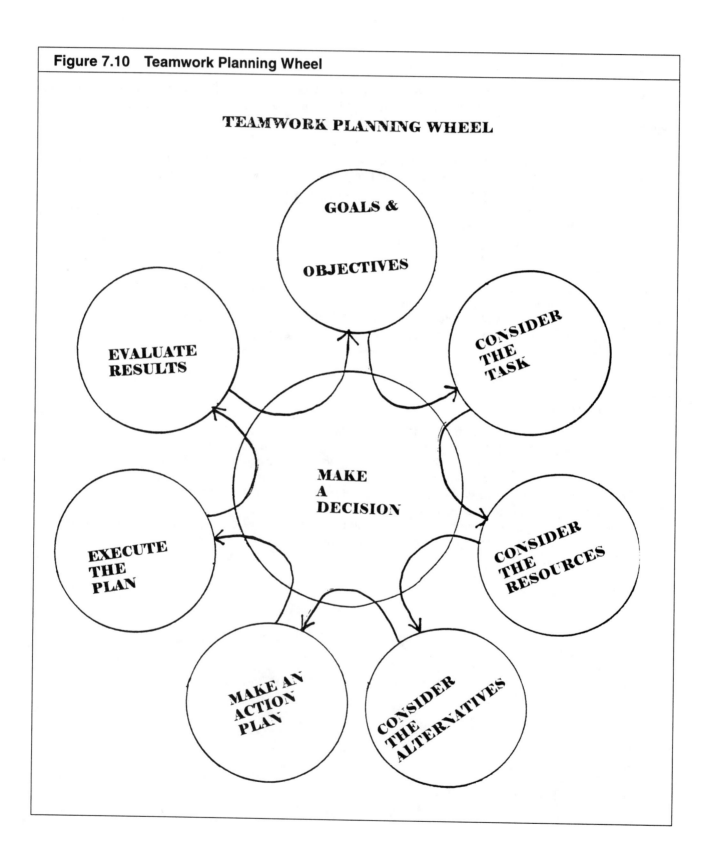

Figure 7.11   Teamwork Handout

Thinking About Teamwork

Teamwork results when interrelated elements bring a group of individuals into cohesive units that function together and work to achieve the organization's goals.

> You must learn how to work together.

> You must learn to play on each other's strengths because that makes the team stronger.

> You must learn to pick up the ball when someone makes a mistake.

Teams should establish:

> their work standards;
> their sequence of work;
> the production process;
> the tools that will be used;
> their schedules in cooperation with the overall needs of the organization.

Attempts should be made to avoid duplication of effort. Teams increase cooperation, spur new ideas, and inspire product quality.

ORGANIZING YOUR TIME

If there is any one thing that we would universally agree upon it would be that we could all use more time. If we think about it, however, we would realize that no one has more time than the next person. We each have twenty-four-hour days, yet some people are able to get so much more done than others. The key is not that they have more time, but rather that they know how to use their time much more efficiently. The following training program will provide both tips and strategies so that your staff will learn how to use its time more efficiently. It is followed by a series of handouts that should help the individual focus on the organization of his or her duties to conserve time. These handouts can also aid troubleshooting because they point out time-wasters and offer some solutions for change.

TIME MANAGEMENT

I. Time Management Is Life Management
  A. Employees need to develop a sense of urgency about tasks
    1. Priorities must be set for tasks
    2. Tasks must be actions that will help organizations reach goals
  B. Priorities will be achieved if there is urgency about tasks
    1. Staff must learn how to complete tasks
    2. Do the most important things first
II. Organizing Tasks Reduces Stress
  A. Stress occurs when the individual believes the demands of a situation are more than can be handled
    1. An internal support system can help overcome this
    2. Rotation of workload and responsibilities can help
  B. Change your perception of stress
    1. Keep goals realistic
    2. List positive achievements
    3. Self-esteem is the foundation of competence
III. Emphasize Effectiveness
  A. Organizations need to evaluate their process
    1. 90% of wasted time can be eliminated with a little common sense
    2. Use information to develop timesaving advantages
  B. Projects change to save time
    1. Use empty space time or downtime to accomplish large projects all at once
    2. Develop plans in advance to be ready for this
IV. Personal Development Is a Springboard to Efficiency
  A. Continuing to learn puts us at an advantage
    1. Develop our skills
    2. Develop our personalities
  B. Balance our lives
    1. Learn to take time for ourselves
    2. Learn to be our own best asset
V. Conclusion
  A. Use aids that will work for you
    1. Technology should help (phone, fax, planners)
    2. Organize work for efficiency
  B. Teamwork helps time management
    1. Working together increases efficiency
    2. Everyone is working for same goals
    3. No one has more time than another; success is proportionate to how well time is utilized and managed

---

Figure 7.12 Organizing Your Time

Training Objective:	To assist staff members in developing organization skills for their time.
Program Purpose:	With the current trend of staff reductions, it has become even more critical to work effectively and efficiently.
Training Methods:	Small group sessions; handouts; hands-on practice on implementing newly found skills.
Training Aids:	Posters; calendars, rolodexes, and other organizer units.
Evaluation:	More tasks are accomplished within the workday.

TIME MANAGEMENT HINTS

1. Respect time and do not waste it. Wasted time decreases the time available for profitable use.
2. Analyze and budget your time. Examine how you spend your time and determine how much you actually need to accomplish tasks. Then budget the time necessary.
3. Do the things you do not like to do *first*. It is a real motivator to accomplish tasks that you do not like.
4. Make a "to do" list and prioritize everything you have to do. Finish each item before you go on to the next. Cross it out—it will make you feel you have accomplished something.
5. Make appointments for specific times.
6. Use the telephone properly. Prepare for each call. List points you want to cover. Keep calls brief and to the point.
7. If you reach voice mail or need to leave a message, leave an action message so the person you are calling will know what you need done. This helps avoid telephone tag.
8. Use a calendar. A pocket calendar, a portable computer catalog, or a program on a PC should be updated daily and reviewed weekly. Be sure to include all appointments, deadlines, and commitments. Use date prompters as necessary.
9. Use a filing system, and keep materials filed daily. Many items can be reused, referred to, and reworked.
10. Record thoughts and ideas on index cards, in a small notebook, or with a tape recorder, as you prefer. Add these into your files as you update them.

Figure 7.13   Time Management Handout

Evaluate your day to see if you are wasting time. Then develop a plan to help organize yourself better.

Schedule

1. How many deadlines do I normally have every day?
2. Are these deadlines self-imposed?
3. Could any of these tasks be postponed? Done another way? Not done at all?
4. How many of these tasks are handled by me only? Can they be done by someone else?
5. What happens if I do not complete these tasks or meet these deadlines?
6. How do I feel at the end of the day? Exhilarated? Tired? Worn out? Satisfied? Frustrated?

Meetings

1. Is this meeting necessary? How else might I accomplish the task?
2. Do participants come well prepared and well organized?
3. Do meetings start and finish on time?
4. Is the meeting's purpose clearly understood?
5. Is there an agenda?
6. Does everyone leave the meeting with action plans that are well defined and agreed upon?

Figure 7.14   Time Management Handout

Setting Priorities

- Devote 80% of your time to the top 20% of your priorities.
- List your major projects for the year. Rearrange them in order of priority.
- Identify your major projects for the month, put them in priority order, and then develop your work schedule for the week.
- Confirm appointments to avoid wasting transit time.
- Control your open-door policy. While a good manager is accessible, you need some uninterrupted time to concentrate and for yourself.
- Use new technologies to help you work smarter.
- Create some quiet time for yourself. You need to recharge.
- Negotiate in person whenever possible with the person who will make the decisions.
- Remember: People will measure you by your accomplishments, your production, not by the number of hours you have worked. Get things done!

Figure 7.15 Work Schedule

Monday	Tuesday	Wednesday	Thursday	Friday	Saturday

Schedule for _____ **Date** _____

8:00 a.m. _____	2:30 p.m. _____
8:15 a.m. _____	2:45 p.m. _____
8:30 a.m. _____	3:00 p.m. _____
8:45 a.m. _____	3:15 p.m. _____
9:00 a.m. _____	3:30 p.m. _____
9:15 a.m. _____	3:45 p.m. _____
9:30 a.m. _____	4:00 p.m. _____
9:45 a.m. _____	4:15 p.m. _____
10:00 a.m. _____	4:30 p.m. _____
10:15 a.m. _____	4:45 p.m. _____
10:30 a.m. _____	5:00 p.m. _____
10:45 a.m. _____	5:15 p.m. _____
11:00 a.m. _____	5:30 p.m. _____
11:15 a.m. _____	5:45 p.m. _____
11:30 a.m. _____	6:00 p.m. _____
11:45 a.m. _____	6:15 p.m. _____
12:00 p.m. _____	6:30 p.m. _____
12:15 p.m. _____	6:45 p.m. _____
12:30 p.m. _____	7:00 p.m. _____
12:45 p.m. _____	7:15 p.m. _____
1:00 p.m. _____	7:30 p.m. _____
1:15 p.m. _____	7:45 p.m. _____
1:30 p.m. _____	8:00 p.m. _____
1:45 p.m. _____	8:15 p.m. _____
2:00 p.m. _____	8:30 p.m. _____
2:15 p.m. _____	8:45 p.m. _____

Project Notes

1.

2.

3.

4.

5.

6.

7.

CUSTOMER SERVICE TRAINING

Customer service, or service to our user communities, is without a doubt one of the major portions of our library staff's job. It is a learned skilled that at times can be frustrating, but it is also the area in which most of us feel most rewarded. It is the vital link between our organization and the people we serve. Each person in the organization is a link in a service chain that searches out, acquires, processes, catalogs, and provides materials, information, and service to our patrons. Only as a complete, interactive team can we serve our users' needs fully and efficiently. Customer expectations are higher than they ever were before, so in libraries we are faced with changing the way all of the employees think about themselves and their patrons.

Institution of a customer service program in the library needs to be done in phases. During the first phase, the library administration must make an audit of the current levels of service in the library. The resulting awareness must include a realization that there will be some things that must change. Next, a commitment to the process must be made by the governing body of the library as well as by the administration. The staff development component is the next phase, in which actual training sessions are held with the staff. Part of the training will be developing the commitment of the staff to the process. Putting the plan into action follows. An evaluation process is an absolute must. Components of it must be from the insiders, but we must also make some tools available to gather input from our customer base. Our quality will be defined by the users, since it is our ability to meet their needs and then go on to exceed their expectations that is the essence of customer service.

Successful organizations have some things in common. There is a strong vision of what library service is all about. Service is a regular discussion item, both formally at meetings and through informal opportunities. There is a balance between the innovations provided, especially the highly technical ones, with a human, user-friendly approach. Staff is carefully recruited, trained, and encouraged to promote good service. Services are marketed to customers, and the quality of these services is not only measured by the customers—the results are also shared with them.

CUSTOMER SERVICE CURRICULUM

I. Introduction
   A. Description of customer service

B. Library's customer service philosophy
II. Customer Service Audit Process
   A. Internal evaluation of what is in place
   B. Community services survey for patrons
III. Ten Steps to Service Success
   A. Recognition of the points of encounter (where employees have contact with the users)
     1. This is where you win or lose users
     2. Observe and analyze service interactions, frequently putting yourself into the role of user
   B. Identify problem areas of service
     1. Service desks as outlets of service
     2. Logistical arrangement of resources
     3. Identify opportunities that stand out and points which need correction
   C. Develop plan of action for implementing changes to improve service
     1. Ideas become solutions to the deficiencies
     2. New approaches are added to improve service
   D. Prioritization of service execution
     1. List the community's needs in order of priority
     2. Establish service goals to meet these priorities
   E. Reallocation of resources to meet new service goals
     1. Financial
     2. Personnel
     3. Equipment, collection
   F. Recruiting other personnel
     1. Criteria for selection of both paid personnel and volunteers must include a potential for good service attitudes
     2. All staff must be amenable to learning
   G. Continued commitment to training
     1. Our technology is constantly changing, and we need to make sure we can help our users learn to use it.
     2. Our users are changing constantly as well, so our training of them will be continual
   H. Communications are well established
     1. Patrons are aware of policies, procedures, and all services
     2. Signs, newsletters, posters, etc., dealing with the library's services are clear, concise, and useful
   I. Follow up execution
     1. Make changes with items that are not working
     2. Implement new plans

    J. Evaluate
      1. Evaluate what went wrong and make changes
      2. Reinforce the positive and applaud success
IV. Good Customer Service Is Critical to Repeat Use
    A. Provide staff with the authority to bend policies using their good judgment so that the customer finds value
      1. Smile
      2. Be polite and tactful
    B. Perception is an all-important aspect of customer service. Users need to receive
      1. prompt service
      2. no hassles
      3. competent assistance
      4. convenient hours and locations
      5. value
V. Conclusion
    A. Libraries can be confusing and intimidating; we have a responsibility to use our expertise to connect our users with the appropriate materials and services
    B. Goals of customer service (suggestions)
      1. Welcome library users and keep them feeling welcome and comfortable in the library
      2. Determine the patron's information needs
      3. Match the library's resources with the user's needs in a timely fashion

---

Figure 7.16 Customer Service Handout

Library philosophy: As a library, we want to provide friendly, responsive, efficient service to all of our users. We will do this by having a caring, respectful, and positive work environment which values all individual talents as we strive to reach our common goal. In order to do this, we continually seek innovative approaches to provide efficient, accurate, and complete information services.

Key element for managers: When employees are favorable toward the organization in which they work and its policies, customers view the quality of service they receive favorably. Internal marketing is a must.

Employees need to make informed judgments.

Employees need to maintain a positive attitude.

Use Customer Service Assessment (Figure 7.17).

Use group discussion activities.

Distribute official customer service policy.

4. Register borrowers and circulate materials in a consistent, understanding, knowledgeable, and informed fashion
5. Have the departing patron want to continue to use the library's services on a regular basis and to become a library supporters in the community

Figure 7.17 Customer Service Assessment			
Please check the appropriate response.			
	Frequently	**Sometimes**	**Never**
1. Project an open, positive, friendly attitude toward every individual.			
2. Respond to complaints in a courteous and sympathetic manner.			
3. Use effective and attentive listening skills.			
4. Ask a telephone caller for permission to be put on hold and thank the caller for waiting when you return.			
5. Follow the transaction through until the customer is satisfied.			
6. Apologize even when it's not your fault.			
7. Provide timely responses to requests.			
8. Give equal consideration to the telephone and in-person customer.			
9. Provide assistance without being asked.			
10. Respond positively—what you can do, not what you cannot do.			
11. Speak clearly at all times.			
12. Show you are courteous. Say "Please" and "Thank you."			
13. Maintain a nonjudgmental attitude toward customers' questions.			
14. Communicate on the level of the customer (no jargon).			
15. Identify the branch/department, give your name, and offer help when answering the telephone.			
16. Acknowledge others for providing good customer service.			

Figure 7.18   Sample Customer Services Policy

City of Meriden
Meriden Public Library
Customer Public Service Policy
Marcia M. Trotta, M.S., Director
Joan S. Edgerly, President
Library Board of Directors

The MERIDEN PUBLIC LIBRARY strives to offer excellent library services to all. In addition to the quality of the facility and the collection, it is equally important that the library staff provide accurate, efficient, and friendly service at all times. Although we often view the patrons as the clientele, it is important to remember that the patron, as a voter and taxpayer, is also the ultimate boss.

The customer service policy is the foundation for all staff interactions with the general public. All other library policies should be interpreted in light of the principles outlined below.

1. The library should offer the same quality of service to all regardless of age, race, sex, nationality, educational background, physical limitations, or any other criteria which may be the source of discrimination.
2. Patrons should be treated as if they are the most important people in the world. They are!
3. Judgment calls should always be made in the patron's favor. Mistakes should always be to the patron's advantage. Staff will not be penalized for errors made in good faith pursuit of this policy
4. Patrons should never be left without an alternative if a staff member is unable to comply with their request (see attached procedures).
5. Staff members should be familiar with and able to articulate library policies as well as explain the rationale behind them.

Demeanor
Demeanor is defined as the way a person looks, speaks, and acts; one's manner of behavior toward others; a personal mode of expressing attitude. Nonverbal demeanor conveys attitude via facial expression and posture just as the tone of voice and choice of words affect a message.

In public service institutions such as the library, it is imperative that every staff/patron interaction is a positive one for the patron. A friendly, helpful demeanor can often ensure a positive experience even when the message conveyed is not a pleasant one.

Staff members are expected to act in a friendly, helpful manner to ensure that the patron will walk away feeling that his or her experience with the library has been a positive one (see attached procedures).

Each staff member, while at work, acts as a representative of the library to each person or group with whom she or he comes in contact. The impression made on the patron profoundly affects the library's image and ongoing support.

Ethics
The needs and requests of library patrons must always be taken seriously and treated with respect. Equal consideration and treatment will be given to users within established guidelines and in a nonjudgmental environment.

All interactions and transactions between a library patron or group of patrons and the library will be considered confidential and will be discussed only in a professional context (such matters include, but are not limited to, registration information, materials selection, loan transaction records, reference questions, patron card status, etc.). Staff should remember that, although the temptation to discuss or share difficult transactions at the public desk is great, such discussion should be limited to the staff lounge or private offices; these details are confidential as well.

Figure 7.18 Continued

Staff members will not offer personal opinions or advice in answer to queries, but will always follow established library practice.

Positive Operating Procedures
1. Be punctual. Service commences at the advertised hour we open. Phones should be answered and workstations staffed when the library opens for the public.
2. Smile.
3. Greet the patron. Acknowledge a patron's presence by looking up and making eye contact or by greeting verbally.
4. Look up and around periodically. Being helpful to patrons takes precedence over desk work; patrons should not be led to think otherwise.
5. Conduct transactions in a helpful, pleasant tone of voice. Keep any impatience, annoyance, or implication of ignorance from your voice. Pretend it is their first visit to the library (if not, it may be their last). It's always better to presume that the patron is unfamiliar with the library.
6. Unless there is a specific discipline problem, do not reprimand or scold patrons.
7. Be jargon free when talking to library patrons.
   a. Avoid library and computer jargon or abbreviations which may be meaningless to the patron (e.g., "delinquency," "reference," "circulation," "ILL," etc.).
   b. Explain to the patron what procedure you will be following if it is not readily apparent (e.g., "I will be contacting another library for the book that you want; it may take several days. When it comes in, we will call to notify you to come and pick it up").

Examples of Situations When Alternative Should Be Offered
(Illustration only, not limitation)
I. Children's Library
   1. If a book is not on the shelf, check the computer, then trucks or books to be shelved; offer to reserve or ILL the material.
   2. If a question cannot be answered from the children's reference collection, refer the patron to adult reference and call ahead to alert them.
II. Circulation Department
   A. Main desk
      1. If a patron forgets his or her card, offer to look it up. Remind patron that the system may be down or that they may need to use an area library, and that carrying the card is important.
      2. If a patron comes up delinquent, suggest some options:
         a. Renew overdue materials if the patron says he or she has them.
         b. Offer to hold the items for three days to allow the patron to clear up the delinquency.
         c. Offer to photocopy needed information if only a few pages.
         d. If a patron has a stop on his or her card, offer a shorter loan period if there is an urgent need for material.
   B. Videos
      1. If a patron has not rewound a video, ask that it please be done next time.
      2. If a snow closing or other emergency might affect the patron's ability to return videos on time to the library, waive the overdue charge.
III. Adult Reference Department
   1. Conduct a proper reference interview: e.g., make sure that you give the patron what he or she wants, not necessarily what was asked for.

Figure 7.18 Continued

---

   a. Clarify what the person really needs. When someone asks you, "Where are the biographies?" ask if they need help finding a particular book.

   b. Follow up whenever possible with "Did you find just what you were looking for?" or "May I help you further?"

2. Never let the patron leave without an answer to his or her question or without a referral to another source. The words "We don't have that here" should always be followed by "But I'll see if I can locate it for you."

   a. Offer to help with equipment and copiers.

   b. Offer to reserve materials.

   c. Offer ILL when possible.

   d. Offer to fill out order form for a new title.

   e. Call another library for information when appropriate.

   f. Give the patron a referral to someone who can answer the question or provide the information.

   g. Never point. Always go to shelf or catalog with the patron.

The following two handouts work well to spark discussion among the participants in customer service training. Figure 7.19 has specific goals and expectations. If these goals are not consistent with those of your library, they should be changed so. In any event, the purpose of such a handout is to indicate that one cannot demand a certain level of behavior from a staff that is not fully aware of what you expect. You must tell them. The case studies that are described in Figure 7.20 can be given to different groups, allowing them fifteen or twenty minutes to discuss the situations. They can then report back to the whole group of participants. It is always a learning experience to see the different ways in which different people tackle the same problem. If you stop to think, you would realize that each of us has numerous customer-inspired stories that would make good case studies. The use of actual situations from your library makes the lessons all the more real to the participants. It gives the administrator a way to illustrate through role-playing the way in which he or she believes that the staff should have dealt with a situation rather than the way in which it was handled. It also creates an opportunity to single out individuals who offered exceptional service. Others will then begin to look to them for advice and model their behavior on that of the one who was outstanding. If group situations do not work well in your library, then by all means use these situations during one-on-one training. Force people to think about good and bad service they have received elsewhere (in libraries and in retail establishments). Occasionally, we all need to be reminded that we are there for the patron (customer) and reinforce our own customer service skills.

Figure 7.19	How to Apply Customer Service Techniques to Service Goals
1. Goal:	To welcome library user and to keep him or her comfortable in the library.
Expectation of staff:	To direct patrons to the appropriate location, approaching them in a friendly, courteous manner if they do not approach you.
Special Considerations:	Libraries can be confusing and intimidating especially to persons with little or no library experience, so be patient and courteous in providing the service. Patrons expect immediate satisfaction. If it is not possible to give it to them, be sure to make the referral in a very helpful way.
2. Goal:	To determine the patron's information needs.
Expectation of staff:	Everyone on the staff should be knowledgeable about location of materials. Patrons should be directed to the staff member best able to help them, in light of the subject and depth of the question.
Special Considerations:	Many patrons have only a vague awareness of what they want, or they ask for something other than what they really want, so queries must be made politely to understand the exact information need. Patrons are not aware of the differences in levels of training of support staff and librarians, so they must be assured they are getting the expert. A librarian with extensive reference interview experience can save much time and frustration for patron and staff.
3. Goal:	To match the library's resources with the user's needs in a timely fashion.
Expectation of staff:	The staff members should link the user with the resource. If they are able, they should teach the users to help themselves (e.g., using an online catalog). If the transaction is not possible with our collection, then proceed to make other arrangements through ILL, etc.
Special Considerations:	Ultimately, the patron will decide which materials to use. Our role is to suggest appropriate selections.
4. Goal:	To register borrowers and circulate materials in a consistent, understanding, knowledgeable, and informed fashion.
Expectation of staff:	The staff must know the library's procedures and policies, as well have a thorough familiarity with the library's circulation system. In addition, the staff needs to maintain a friendly, helpful, positive, and tactful posture in patron transactions. The customer service approach comes into play especially when problem-solving, Overdue fines, renewals, reserves, and lost materials need to be handled firmly yet fairly. Furthermore, staff must be empowered to bend rules based on their judgment.
Special Considerations:	A good level of cooperation and trust must be developed among the staff so that they can support one another in any given situation.
5. Goal:	To have the departing patron want to continue to use the library's service on a regular basis and to have them become library supporters in the community.
Expectation of staff:	Interactions will vary with circumstances, but it is a good rule to ask if the patron found what he or she was looking for. Patrons should be bid good day, and programs should be promoted. Bookmarks with information about the library or about Friends of the Library are good ideas.
Special Considerations:	Patrons who leave with a positive feeling are more likely to become repeat users.

Figure 7.20   Sample Cases for Practicing Customer Service Skills

1. How would you handle this situation, remembering that you want to encourage the child to become a good customer?
A child, age ten, comes to the desk to check out some books. His mother is standing behind him with an unpleasant look on her face. The child does not have his card with him. You look it up on the computer to find that he has five different cards registered to him. He is also blocked from checking out more materials because he has not returned other books.

2. Equipment within the library—what to do?
A college-age customer comes to you for help. He does not have any money, but needs to copy some material. Each page cost ten cents. What can you do to help?

3. New borrower
A woman comes into the library and she wants to check out materials; however, she does not have a library card or proof of identification with her. What do you do?

4. Checking out reference material
A student arrives at your desk and desperately needs to take home a reference book for a term paper due in the morning. He promises to have the book back at 8 a.m. You allow the reference book to be taken out of the library, and it does not come back at 8 a.m. The student doesn't answer the phone when you call, and the book does not come back until 4:30 in the afternoon. How do you handle the situation?

5. Lost materials
The patron insists that a book that is outstanding on his record has been returned. You verify that the shelves have been searched and the book is not in the library. What do you do?

Figure 7.21 Things to Remember About Customer Service

Customers should never be inconvenienced because of policies that are known only to employees.

A customer should not have to repeat a request or complaint to several employees before having it resolved.

Quality service means never having to say, "That's not my job."

Customers cannot be satisfied until they are not dissatisfied. Your first service priority should be to eliminate, as far as possible, causes of customer dissatisfaction.

A few quick successes do not add up to sustained service. Quality is the result of a *systematic* approach which takes time, attention, direction, and effort. It is *consistent.*

Barriers to Customer Services—Please Avoid

1. Inadequate communication between departments.
2. Employees are not appreciated, recognized, or rewarded for quality efforts and service.
3. Understaffing. Quality customer service is dependent on relationships and interaction.
4. Low morale and low team spirit.
5. Inadequate technical and computer equipment or systems.
6. Inadequate training and skill development.
7. Lack of support from those who oversee operation (agency, board, governments).
8. Organizational policies and procedures not set up to meet the needs of the customers.

Customer's Criteria for Service

1. Reliability: The ability to provide what is promised, dependably and accurately.
2. Responsiveness: Prompt service.
3. Authority: Credibility of knowledge.
4. Empathy: The degree of caring and individual attention shown.
5. Physical Appearance: The physical appearance of the facility and the equipment; convenient and at-
            tractive arrangement of materials.

8 EVALUATING STAFF PERFORMANCE

Every organization, whether a nonprofit or a profit-making venture, needs evaluation procedures to measure its effectiveness. Performance appraisals are necessary on an annual basis, and they are best when they are developed in collaborative planning sessions between the supervisors and employees. Goals and objectives need to be set for the upcoming year, and the training offered should fit these. While there are many good books available on the subject of performance—most notably Sullivan and Stueart's *Performance Analysis and Appraisal*—there are some points that should be highlighted here so that performance evaluation techniques can be tied in with the evaluation process that is a necessity in staff development.

Good performance evaluations will measure the individual's performance on the job in comparison with the job requirements that were listed on the description for it when the employee was hired. The supervisor must be able to assess the quality of the individual's performance and recommend whether the individual is to receive a promotion or a demotion, a salary increase, or special training or retraining. It is the supervisor's responsibility to understand what the employee's potential is, and how it fits into the institution's goal.

Typical standards of employee performance are quality and quantity (how well? how many?); the desired effect or impact (has the employee completed the job? to what degree of accuracy? were deadlines met?); and meeting standards (was the work accomplished in cooperation with others? has the employee been able to adapt to the needs of the job at hand?).

The results of performance appraisal are traditionally used to provide a means of praise and recognition or constructive criticism and assistance for the employee. Supervisors use the exercise as a way of reinforcing organizational objectives and expectations, and they should focus on the employee's potential for improvement and development. As in any good communications process, the employee should be given a forum during this review to express needs, concerns, and questions.

In addition to the formal process of appraisal, supervisors have other means of evaluation at their disposal. These include on-the-job observation, specific opportunities to apply training knowledge, and demonstrations to other employees.

In particular, evaluation should be done as projects are in process, since ongoing feedback helps keep projects on the right track, Staff development programs are certainly included in this category. You use evaluation to measure the effectiveness of each training session, as well as of the overall program, on a semiannual basis. You should be looking at how well your program is able to transfer information from the trainer(s) to the participants and what difference in operations has resulted from the training. All trainers worth their salt will also want to evaluate how well they taught the necessary information. As the library administrator, you are going to want to keep yourself aware of the work of all of the trainers. You will want to judge them from a formal standpoint on how they transferred data and whether employees were then able to apply their newly acquired knowledge. You will also want to pay careful attention to employee feedback on the training to evaluate whether particular trainers are in tune with the needs of the participants. We need to keep in mind that good, overall evaluation procedures will make our programs more effective and will increase not only our level of knowledge but also our library's credibility.

THE NEED FOR EVALUATION

Evaluations provide the means by which we are able to judge the success of our training program. There are three primary aspects of training evaluation. The first is a precourse entry evaluation which can zero in on the training or knowledge level of the group on any particular subject. This provides the basis for the session. It is not necessarily the needs assessment that was discussed earlier, but certainly the picture that one is able to derive from that process is helpful prior to developing the program. Simply stated, it might consist of a few questions that the trainer asks his or her audience before getting into the course material. For example, the trainer might say, "How many of you have had an unpleasant experience at a store recently?" and ask for a show of hands. A follow-up question ("What was your reaction?" or "Will you go back to that store?") can then elicit comments and give the trainer some insight into whether the participants are able to distinguish between good and bad customer service. This exercise can be viewed as a pretest and will give the trainer important information on the audience's background, attitudes and experience and will launch the workshop on track.

Second, continuing course evaluation checks on conditions that can be adjusted or changed as necessary while the workshop is being held. Some of these conditions include the pace at which the workshop is being offered; the level of the material that is being used; the quality of any audiovisual aids (are they clear? focused? etc.); the amount of participation from the audience (are they responding? asking questions? nodding in agreement?); and the course logistics (room temperature, break times, seating arrangements).

And finally, the postcourse evaluation views the overall effectiveness of the training program. This should be done as soon after the program is complete as possible so that the information is fresh, but it should also be done after those trained have been able to apply their newly learned skills.

When evaluating participant reactions, you should be careful to pay attention to adverse reactions to the facilities and room arrangements. Although not directly associated with the training, they can affect the participants' attitudes toward the program itself. Anything that can be done to make the participants comfortable will aid in their capacity to learn. Program content should be evaluated in terms of coverage of the topic, on whether it met the objectives of the course, and if it increased the participants' knowledge. One of the best means of evaluating content is through the use of a questionnaire which rates on a scale. This type of evaluation of content is important to improve program material.

Evaluation of the trainer needs to be done on a serious level by the administrator to assess whether he or she has effectively met the course objectives. Good trainers will be evaluating themselves and should be willing to share their thoughts with you. Trainers can word questions on written evaluations to provide some of this much needed feedback. For example, participants should be asked to answer yes or no to questions like "Did the trainer use clear examples?" "Was each point covered with enough detail?" or "Did the trainer hold your interest?" The more detailed your questions are, the more specific will be the data that you have to improve further efforts.

Administrators, and in some cases trainers, are also going to need to evaluate knowledge gain and behavioral changes. Written and oral tests are sometimes appropriate to see if people actually learned the material that was presented; however, the best results can be gained from performance testing which goes a step beyond finding out if the participants learned the material. Performance testing evaluates if they are using it in a particular manner.

Evaluating behavior changes is a means to determine the distinction between learning and performing. This is best done by comparing levels of performance to performance levels preceding the trainings. Ultimately, the most critical evaluation is to see the impact from the individual training on the overall organization.

Once the training programs and the evaluation process are completed, the supervisor or staff development coordinator should be ready to report the results of the training process to those at all levels of concern in the organization, and indeed outside it. Reporting results helps clarify training skills and procedures and can also aid the participants in determining additional training needs. Written reports should be clear and to the point. They should include the needs which you expect to be met after the training session; a summary of the training that was offered; a statement which answers the question "Were the needs met?" and an identification of additional training needs.

Once your library has a staff development process in place, it will become natural for the evaluation of staff performance to be enhanced by evaluating the actual results of the programs. The following pages provide a reminder of why we evaluate and what type of learning results we can measure. Paying attention to this aspect of the process is as important as any other portion of the program.

It is also crucial that we remember that one of the best ways of getting people to participate is to make them feel part of the larger organization. The supervisor's evaluation is key in this area, helping them be perceived as part of the organization rather than exempt from the process. As administrators, we are not above the need to be evaluated, and we must take time out to reflect on our own strengths and weaknesses. Our involvement in the process is what may spark other staff members to become enthusiastic.

WHY EVALUATE?
- To determine whether the needs of the participants have been met
- To determine whether the needs of the organization have been met
- To justify the program
- To establish credibility
- To adapt the program if it is not functioning to meet the needs

METHODS OF EVALUATION

Quantitative
   Number of sessions
   Number of people trained
   Which programs attracted the most people
Trainees' Reactions to
   Instruction
   Content
   Method
   Organization
Learning
   Achievement of objectives
   Verification of competence to perform
   Tests and practice sessions
Performance
   Measures individual performance on the job
   Determines application to on-the-job situations
   Examines behavioral changes
Results
   Impact of training on service to patrons
   Organizational effectiveness (cost down, morale up, lower absenteeism, productivity up, better-satisfied clients, increased usage, fewer complaints)

There is no question that any new innovation—be it a change in the way a task is approached, a new piece of equipment to do the job, a change to an electronic or CD-ROM data base instead of hard copy—will be met with some resistance by a few members of the staff. It is human nature to resist change; we are comfortable with that which is familiar. In every workplace, we will always have those who say, "We've always have done it that way, so why change?" or "We tried that and it did not work." It is the responsibility of the library director to provide the staff, and in some cases, the board of directors, with all of the pros and cons of changes. When people are able to understand the benefits or even the necessity of making the change, their reactions will ultimately overcome the negatives and the resistance. Many people are negative when they do not understand the rationale behind the change, are not able to envision the benefits or fear that their tasks may become more difficult. In fact they may be shown that new methods of working eliminate some tedious and repetitive aspects of their work. They often will become the strongest supporters of the change after you take the time to explain things and ask them to help you implement the changes. The example given here will provide some strategies that can be useful in accomplishing this.

Figure 8.1   Supervisor's Self-Evaluation Checklist

1. What is your personal attitude about the library? Do you think that your attitude affects your ability to supervise others?

2. Do you think that your immediate supervisor is competent?

3. Are you performing your administrative/supervisory functions well?

4. When was the last time you appraised your own performance? Were you objective and honest with yourself?

5. When was the last time you were evaluated by your supervisor? Did you agree with the evaluation?

6. Do your subordinates respect your leadership and technical capabilities?

7. What is your relationship with other supervisors in the library?

8. Do you readily accept new responsibilities?

9. Are you open-minded about suggestions for improvements?

10. Is there any reason to believe that your work is ineffective or not up to standard?

11. Do you participate in opportunities for continuing education?

12. Are you considered to possess a high degree of integrity?

Figure 8.2   Checklist for Rating Employees

1. Technical Ability
   a. understands all phases of work
   b. knows how to use equipment
   c. has knowledge of all operations
   d. can detect own errors
   e. can take corrective action
   f. communicates well
2. Dependability
   a. follows instruction
   b. meets most deadlines
   c. cross-checks results
   d. is flexible with scheduling
3. Personality
   a. gets along well with fellow workers
   b. is willing to help others
   c. is cooperative
   d. attempts to resolve disputes quickly
4. Productivity
   a. maintains a good level of output
   b. has a minimum of wasted effort
   c. revises methods that cause problems or errors
5. Attitude
   a. overcomes work difficulties
   b. is a good team worker
   c. respects supervisors
   d. willing to train others
   e. respects and appreciates customers and their needs
6. Attendance/Punctuality
   a. has minimal absentee record
   b. is flexible in scheduling
   c. calls in when ill
   d. starts and finishes on time consistently
   e. reports promptly to work after break or lunch
7. Attention to Work Environment
   a. has a neat workstation
   b. properly disposes of trash and recycles
   c. stores materials carefully
   d. keeps equipment in good order
   e. observes safety rules
8. Adaptability
   a. is supportive of changes
   b. learns new methods and equipment
   c. shows a willingness to be retrained
   d. respects authority

Figure 8.2 Continued

9. Potential
    a. seeks to be recognized for expertise
    b. studies and trains for promotion; is ambitious
    c. trains or leads others
    d. is motivated
10. Commitment
    a. to the organization
    b. to the profession

Figure 8.3 Employee Evaluation

The purpose of the employee evaluation is to take a personal inventory of the individual, pinpointing both strengths and weakness. The employee and the supervisor should be able to reach some consensus and should develop a practical empowerment program which includes expectations and goals. All categories should be discussed.

Categories of judgment
1. Accuracy: how much supervision is required?
2. Alertness: what is the ability to learn and understand?
3. Creativity: is there a talent for having new ideas and for finding new and better ways of doing things?
4. Personality: is the person suited to the job, and how does he or she relate to customers, other employees, supervisors?
5. Attendance: is the employee punctual and reliable?
6. Housekeeping: is the work area orderly and clean?
7. Dependability: are required jobs done well with a minimum of supervision?
8. Job knowledge: doe the employee have information concerning duties necessary to perform the job satisfactorily.
9. Productivity: how much does the employee produce in a given day?
10. Drive: is there a desire to attain goals?

Figure 8.4   Overcoming Employee Resistance to Change

All managers will face employees who are finding it difficult to accept change at some time during their careers. A good method of counteracting these attitudes is to prepare for the reactions by anticipating them. Here is a list of some common reactions and attitudes of which we should be aware.

1. Premature judgment: "Before you go any further, it won't work."
2. Cursory evaluation: Only the most obvious factors are considered, and detail is ignored.
3. Self-serving assumptions: Jumping to conclusions that the person finds desirable; ignoring the actual facts.
4. Single-value judgments: Only one criterion is judged.
5. Either/or: Oversimplified judgment instead of values is used to evaluate change.
6. Inaccurate value scales: An inaccurate scale of values is used to evaluate change.
7. Sweeping generalizations: Stereotypes are offered of people, things and ideas without regard to actual facts.
8. Semantic approach: Certain words or phrases are used to cause an emotional response that could result in unfortunate, inconclusive, or inadequate judging of facts.

The supervisor who can anticipate the employees' response might be able to counteract the negatives at the outset and will be better able to overcome resistance.

Figure 8.5   Evaluation for Training Program

Successful Staff Development

Please rate the following on a scale of 1 to 5, with 1 being the lowest and 5 being the highest.

1. Content of materials   _____

2. Handouts   _____

3. Style of delivery   _____

4. Adequate time   _____

5. Questions answered   _____

6. Workshop met expectations   _____

7. Other   _____

Comments: _____

_____

_____

_____

_____

9 BEYOND SALARIES: REWARDING EFFECTIVE PERFORMANCE

Salary increases and monetary and fringe benefits are important to everyone, but they certainly are not the only reason people become motivated to do their best on the job. Both experience and research indicate that most people need to feel positive about the job they are doing. People who feel capable and competent in performing their jobs will be highly motivated to continue to perform them well. It is important that supervisors encourage these feelings of competence. Every good manager should be aware of the potential benefits of praise and positive feedback. These are a way to inspire and motivate people, who like to know that their efforts, as well as the results of these efforts, are truly appreciated. The praise must be consistent with the expectations that the supervisor has for the employee, however, or it becomes quite easy to shrug off the praise as inconsequential. On the other hand, it is also true that most people want to know when they are not performing properly, but they want to know in a way that does not force them to swallow their pride or lose their self-respect. If criticized before other staff members or not given the chance to save face, they may become resentful; rather than improving the employee's performance, the feedback may only worsen it. Giving effective criticism is a valuable skill that every supervisor should develop as an important part of management responsibilities.

As crucial as it is to give someone a pat on the back, other kinds of recognition are valuable as well. Employees should be able to accrue benefits from their achievements and from the satisfactory acceptance of particular responsibilities. Recognition comes in many forms. Beyond simple praise, employees should be encouraged, when appropriate, to assume more challenging work within the library. Promotions are not always possible, but some symbols of the new status often work just as well and can be had for very little money. A change in title, a new name badge, and the relocation of work space are but a few examples of what might be included within this realm of possibilities.

Any praise or rewards given to employees should be additional recognition rather than a substitute for raises or promotions due the employee. There are many times, however, when we as library administrators do not have control of the funding for these positions. The governing body may decide that no raises are to be given, and our hands are tied insofar as giving employees much-needed pay increases. So, we must remain sensitive to this scenario and recognize that giving an employee a certificate for good work under these circumstances most likely will not be appreciated. On the other hand, if the reward is made in addition to the other raises, vacation days, etc., that are due the employee, it can do wonders. The recognition has to be a sign of appreciation rather than a substitute for a raise for it to be effective.

Recognition is actually the final piece of an internal marketing strategy which can be used to enhance the pride and the commitment of the employee within the organization. Employees should realize that their achievements will bring pride and recognition to the library as well as themselves and that they are appreciated for this. This awareness of their personal contributions links the employees to the tradition and heritage of the library. In addition, the proper use of the recognition of one employee will create pride in all the staff members. They will feel good to know that their library employs the best. Recognition has some other hidden benefits: nothing generates success more than success. Recognition possibilities encourage further creativity and productivity.

There are many strategies for providing recognition. One of the simplest ways is to convey recognition of the achievement verbally at the time of the performance or within a reasonable time thereafter. An example might be, "Jane, you handled the public beautifully during the power outage. Many of them might have panicked in the darkness, but you kept your cool, and they followed suit. Nice work." Providing this type of recognition within earshot of other staff members, or indeed of the public, is appropriate, and the employee usually will be most appreciative of your effort to single them out. Sometimes, it is effective to render that recognition more than once. An achievement like the above might be rephrased and presented to the governing board or repeated in an article in the newspaper commending Jane. This provides the opportunity for others to join in the applause. At other times, it might be better to call the employee aside and commend her in private.

Employees who feel appreciated by their organization and colleagues will be better motivated to do a more conscientious job. A little pat on the back once in a while can do wonders for productivity at no cost and with little effort. Staff needs recognition to provide security and a sense of belonging and to improve overall morale.

Rewards are important to provide the psychological motivation for the staff. Once good behaviors have been established, a relatively small amount of reinforcement will help maintain their momentum. The other thing to remember about reinforcement is that it is more powerful the more immediate it is and that continuous reinforcement maintains good behavior. Both excellence and progress are appropriate matters for recognition.

There are several products that can be purchased that are intended to provide recognition. They are inspiring and attractive, but their cost may be out of reach for most library budgets. The recognition gift does not need to be expensive in order to be effective, however. In fact, many have no cost at all. The most important thing is that the item is appropriate for the given situation and for the particular employee who is receiving it. Anything personalized with the name, date, and occasion is always valued.

While it marks achievement, recognition has the added potential of being the first step in another cycle of achievement. Staff development keeps people from burning out. It is a never-ending process. If we are going to deliver quality services, we must support this process on an ongoing basis. Staff development is an investment in our futures; it should be a library priority, but it must also be a responsibility shared between the employer and the employee. The toughest thing about effective management is that you must keep on doing it in order to be effective, and you must teach others in a supervisory position to do it as well.

Those who are in management must remember that change begins with us. Management is a difficult job, and we cannot do it alone. We must surround ourselves with well-trained staff members who can be of help. Changing your organization is not a single, ultimate solution; it is, in fact, a never-ending process which keeps on presenting different sets of problems. Managing the process of change through effective staff development is a major part of the solution.

IMPORTANCE OF NONMONETARY RECOGNITION

People like to feel that they are succeeding in what they are doing, and some recognition of their abilities and achievements will go a long way in satisfying them. Increases in financial incentives do not necessarily result in more productivity; performance empowerment can be improved by status symbols and awards. External recognition of one's effectiveness reinforces faith in one's own assessment of good performance.

Recognition is one of the most effective ways of managing people. It simply responds to our basic human nature—we all want to be told that we are doing a good job. And it can be simply that. A smile, an inquiry about a family member, a sincere "You did a great job!" doesn't cost anything, yet it can go a long way toward making a staff member feel appreciated and a part of the team. The following are examples of some appropriate times and ways to provide staff recognition.

1. A change in job title or a promotion.
2. A change in workstation or office location.
3. An article in a newsletter.
4. A certificate or plaque.
5. A commendation or letter from the board of trustees.
6. Increased authority.
7. Representing library or administration at a function.
8. Creation of legends or stories about achievements that become part of the library traditions.

Figure 9.1   Ways to Give Recognition

1. A handshake from the director or board president before an audience.
2. An engraved certificate.
3. A mention or an article in a newsletter or other publication.
4. A press release in local papers, including photo.
5. A plaque, desktop pen and pencil set, or paperweight to display the achievement.
6. A flower or small memento that is appropriate for the particular person.
7. A simple thank you, oral or written.
8. A letter of appreciation in a personnel file.
9. An appreciation luncheon or tea.
10. A pin that recognizes achievement.
11. A special parking space.
12. A public acknowledgment that the staff member is responsible for the success.
13. A limited edition of a mug, book bag, or other library memento.
14. A promotion.
15. Business cards or personalized stationery.
16. Recognition from someone else who has power (mayor or other elected officials, state association).
17. Larger work area.
18. A more challenging job as an opportunity for growth.
19. An opportunity to represent the library publicly at a significant function or occasion.

CONCLUSION

There are some basic concepts that you may want to carry away from reading this book. First, in order to empower others, you must first empower yourself. You, the director, must exhibit continuing development and learning, openness to new ideas, willingness to try them, and skill in melding them into the traditions and mission of the library. Second, you must convey to your staff your firm and abiding belief that change, though inevitable, can be managed and shaped so that it is a positive force rather than a confusing and negative one. It is basic to your program of staff development that you articulate constantly the truth that staff development must be a given for every member of the organization—professionals, support staff, trustees, and volunteers—and that this requirement will only increase in the decades to come.

Figure 9.2 Sample Opportunities to Provide Recognition

1. Achievement of a particular goal.
2. Reaching a quota, breakthrough, or project completion.
3. Submission of a cost-saving suggestion.
4. A year of perfect attendance or an extensive on-time record.
5. Community service, representing self or library.
6. Professional service (e.g., on library association executive board) representing library.
7. Suggestion of a new way to provide a service or do a routine task.
8. Feedback from the users about a person.
9. Completion of a formal training program.
10. Leadership during a crisis.

10 RESOURCES

There are many more resources to help us with our staff development programs than we think. It takes some research into our local community to locate them, but the time spent is well worth it. The following pages will provide some concrete suggestions of where to go for help and some thoughts about getting started as you look for particular resources within your own community.

SUGGESTED READINGS FOR ADMINISTRATORS

LIBRARY SPECIFIC

Bessler, Joanne M. *Putting Service into Library Staff Training: A Patron-Center Guide.* Chicago: American Library Association, 1994.

Caputo, Janette. *Stress and Burnout in Library Service.* Phoenix, Arizona: Oryx, 1991.

Castelyn, Mary. *Promoting Excellence: Personal Management and Staff Development in Libraries.* New Providence, N.J.: Saturn, 1992.

Gertgag, Alice, and Edwin Beckerman. *Administration of the Public Library.* Metuchen, New Jersey: Scarecrow Press, 1994.

Rubin, Richard. *Human Resource Management in Libraries.* New York: Neal-Schuman, 1991.

Stueart, Robert, and Barbara Moran. *Library Management*, 4th ed. Littleton, Colorado: Libraries Unlimited, 1993.

MANAGEMENT AND BUSINESS ORIENTED

Although we can learn from one another in the profession, it is equally important that we take advantage of the tremendous amount of material that has been developed for other nonprofits and for businesses. The advice and techniques that are included in these sources can easily be adapted to suit the particular needs of your library. I would not be surprised to learn that your collection has many of these right on your shelves.

Allen, Kathleen. *Time and Information Management That Really Works!* Lincolnwood, Illinois: NTC Business Books, 1995.

Bailey, Gerald. *One Hundred One Activities for Creating Effec-*

tive Technology Staff Development. New York: Scholastic, 1994.

Brew, Angela. *Directions in Staff Development.* Houston, TX: Open U Press, 1995.

Drucker, Peter. *Managing for the Future.* New York: Penguin Group, 1992.

Frank, Milo. *How to Run a Successful Meeting—In Half the Time.* New York: Simon and Schuster, 1989.

Kirby, Tess. *The Can-Do Manager.* New York: American Management Association, 1989.

Klabnick, Joan. *Rewarding and Recognizing Employees: Ideas for Individuals, Teams, and Managers.* New York: Irwin, 1995.

Lawrence, C. Edward. *How to Handle Staff Misconduct.* New York: Carwin, 1994.

Lockwood, Fred. *How to Present and Evaluate Flexible Learning Materials.* Kogan, 1995.

Martin, Don. *Teamthink.* New York: Dulton, 1993.

Marvin, Bill. *From Turnover to Teamwork: How to Build and Retain a Customer-Oriented Workforce.* New York: Wiley, 1994.

Mullins, Terry. *Staff Development Programs: A Guide to Evaluation.* New York: Carwin, 1994.

Rodriguez, Lori. *Manual of Staff Development.* New York: Mosby, 1995.

Worthington, E. R. *People Investments: How to Make Your Hiring Decisions Pay Off for Everyone.* New York: Gasis, 1993.

JOURNALS

All good library administrators keep themselves abreast of the latest developments in the field by reading a variety of publications that are produced for our profession. These should include your state and regional publication as well as, but not limited to, *American Libraries, Bottom Line, Library Administration and Management, Library Journal,* and *Wilson Library Bulletin.*
In addition, these three sources are particularly helpful:

Training and Development Journal
   American Society of Training and Development
   1640 King Street Box 1443
   Alexandria, Virginia 22331
   703–683–8100

Workforce Training News
Enterprise Communications
1483 Chain Bridge Road 202
McLean, Virginia 22101

Working Together
Dartneil Corp.
4660 Ravenswood Ave.
Chicago, Illinois 60640

ASSOCIATIONS

Again, library administrators should be members of their state and regional associations, as well as of the American (or Canadian) Library Association. In addition to holding membership themselves, administrators should encourage membership among eligible employees. Many libraries are able to include membership dues as a legitimate professional development expense, and should do so if able. Furthermore, all staff should be encouraged to participate fully in these associations, attend their meetings and conferences, and serve on various committees and task forces. These are excellent opportunities to broaden staff expertise and knowledge, often at an incredibly reasonable cost.

Membership and networking with other organizations in the community is another opportunity that library administrators should not overlook as a way of encouraging professional growth. Participation in the Chamber of Commerce of your town allows you to join in the seminars they offer. A hidden advantage of such a membership is the networking that you will be able to do with other members of the business community. You might then be able to find out what types of training they are doing and perhaps piggyback onto it. An organization may see this as a way to make an appropriate donation to the library. Another advantage might be that they might lend an executive for a day so that the person could be a volunteer trainer. Other civic-minded organizations that are good investments for membership are Rotary Clubs, Kiwanis, and Lions. These groups, too, can provide support and assistance to your staff development program. Another important part of this approach is what our libraries are able to do for these organizations. Our staffs have specialized skills and can provide services that the businesses might not be able to get otherwise. The opportunities for you to create partnerships with them are there, and in my experience they are all worth the effort.

Three organizations that have fine recommendations for staff development, and equally respected reputations, that would be of use to you are:

American Management Association
135 West 50th Street
New York, New York 10020–1201
212–586–8100

This association sponsors forums worldwide and also publishes books and program manuals that help administrators promote the development and growth of their staffs.

ICMA
777 North Capitol Street NE
Suite 500
Washington, D.C. 20002–4201
202–289–4264

This association specializes in working with county and municipal employees. They offer many correspondence courses and training seminars.

Non-Profit Management Association
315 West 9th Street, Suite 1100
Los Angeles, California 90015

This association provides networking for individuals who work in nonprofit areas.

PEOPLE RESOURCES

American Library Association
50 East Huron Street
Chicago, Illinois 60611
312–944–6780

The Office of Personnel Resources and the Library Administration and Management Association are especially committed to issues relating to librarianship, career goals, and development.

Council of Consulting Organizations
521 5th Avenue, 35th Floor
New York, New York 10175–3598
212–697–9693
This is a group of consultants who work in consulting firms or are private consultants on various topics. Their expertise is extensive, but the cost might be prohibitive.

Talent Banks
It is important that you make contacts within your community, either through the Chamber of Commerce or other resources, to locate "Executives on Loan" who may be able to help you with staff development. Service clubs may also have these listings.

R.S.V.P. (Retired Service Volunteer Program) is another effective resource.
Coordinate with other organizations and agencies to do programs cooperatively or swap trainers among your own organizations.

TOOLS FOR TRAINERS AND RECOGNITION RESOURCES

Career Track Seminars on Tape
MS2 3083 Center Green Drive
Boulder, Colorado 80301–5408
In addition to sponsoring seminars, this company distributes both video and audio cassettes on a broad range of training topics.

Motivation!
720 International Parkway
P.O. Box 450939
Sunrise, Florida 33345–0939
A collection of items that can be used to boost morale and keep customers informed.

Dinn Brothers Recognition Awards
68 Winter Street
Holyoke, Massachusetts 01041–9981
1–800–828–3466
A collection of materials that can be used to increase productivity and improve safety as well as recognize success.

INDEX

Achievement, 19
Adult learners, 7, 12, 22
Attributes of effective
    trainers, 27, 28, 34
Audiovisual aids, 50, 51

B

Behavior changes 47, 91–92
Bibliographies, 25
Brainstorming, 23
Breakout groups, 23
Budget, sample, 20, 21

C

Case studies, 24
Commitment, ix, 2, 27, 41,
    47, 57
Communications, 6, 24,
    58–65
Community
    cooperation, 2
    goodwill, 3
    needs, ix
Competence, 1, 4, 99
Content, 33
Coordinator, Staff
    Development, 19–20
Costs, 20, 25, 47
Customer, 5
Customer Services, 78–87

D

Delegation, 22, 27, 31
Developmental needs, 2
Discussion, 23, 31

E

Employee recognition,
    See Recognition
Empowerment, 31, 101

Evaluation, 15, 89–97
    methods, 93
Expectations, 10, 14

F

Facilitator, 23
Feedback, 27, 53, 99

G

Goals, 10, 47

H

Handouts, 25
Honorarium, 21
Human Resources, 31

I

Icebreaker, 23
Image, 5
Internal Marketing, 4, 5, 6,
    100

J

Job
    descriptions, 48
    satisfaction, 8
    training, 49–52

L

Leadership, 31, 52, 54–56
Learning
    lifelong, 1
    methods, 7
    objectives, 10, 25
    techniques, 7, 22
Lecture, 24

M

Management
    responsibility, ix, 2, 52
    techniques, iv, 52–56, 101
Memberships, 107
Mentor relationships, 39–42
Mission, 4, 5, 32
Morale, 98
Motivation, 19, 21, 31, 38,
    99, 100

N

Needs assessment, 10, 13, 57,
    90

O

Objectives, 10–11
Organizational identity, 6
Orientation, 66

P

Partnerships, 107
Performance
    reviews, 48, 87, 89–97
    standard, 11, 25, 47, 89
    contacts, 4
    development, 14, 40
Planning process, 9
Practice, 11
Presentations, 32, 33
Priorities, 10
Problem solving, 23, 54
Product, 3
Productivity, 9, 100
Program design, 11, 25
Public Library Services, 3
Public relations, 3, 5

Q

Quality of service, 14

Question and Answer
    sessions, 23

R

Recognition, 7, 41, 89, 99–
    103
Reinforcement techniques,
    19, 21, 25, 40
Resource materials, 25, 26,
    33
Role modeling, 39

S

Self-Image, 36–37
Service, 3
Skills, 1, 11

Staff attitude, 3
Staff development
    coordination, 19
    definition, 2
    foundations, x, 2
    process, 15
Staff performance, 3
Staff relationships, 3, 4
Standards, ix, 7, 47
Survey method, 13

T

Team building, 32, 55, 68–73
Time
    management, 73–77
    requirements, 25
Trainer evaluation, 90

Trainer selection, 14, 22, 25,
    28, 34, 35
Training
    hints, 29, 33, 49
    outline, 30
    topics, 57–59

V

Vision, 5, 9, 31

W

Work environment, xi, 39, 69
Workplace, attitude toward,
    3